D0580669

MORE Boredom BUSTERS

OVER 50 AWESOME ACTIVITIES
FOR CHILDREN AGED 7 YEARS +

CAROLINE FERNANDEZ

CICO kidz

This book is dedicated to my three busy children, who inspire me to bust kid boredom with engagement.

Acknowledgments

I would like to express my gratitude to the teams at CICO Books and Thomas Allen & Sons who helped bring this book to life (and to bookstores). Specifically, I would like to thank Cindy Richards, Carmel Edmonds, and Clare Sayer for their guidance and editorial support.

Published in 2015 by CICO Kidz
An imprint of Ryland Peters & Small
341 E 116th St, New York NY 10029
20–21 Jockey's Fields, London WC1R 4BW
www.rylandpeters.com

10 9 8 7 6 5 4 3 2

Text copyright © Caroline Fernandez 2015
Design and photography © CICO Kidz 2015

The author's moral rights have been asserted. All rights reserved. No part of this publication may be reproduced, stored in a retrieval system, or transmitted in any form or by any means, electronic, mechanical, photocopying, or otherwise, without the prior permission of the publisher.

A CIP catalog for this book is available from the Library of Congress and the British Library.

ISBN: 978-1-78249-199-6

Printed in China

Editor: Clare Sayer
Designer: Alison Fenton
Photographer: Martin Norris
Stylist: Sophie Martell
Templates: Stephen Dew

In-house editor: Carmel Edmonds
In-house designer: Fahema Khanam
Art director: Sally Powell
Production controller: Mai-Ling Collyer
Publishing manager: Penny Craig
Publisher: Cindy Richards

Contents

Introduction 6

Chapter 1:
Spring 8

Washer Necklaces 10
Paper Chain People 12
T-shirt Apron 14
Think of Me Tea Card 17
Handprint Tree 20
Gym Bag Sock Buddies 22
Spring Basket 24
Découpage Tiles 26
Potato Stamp Stationery 28
Cotton Ball Sheep 30
Homemade Bird Feeder 32
Sock Monsters 34
Family Photo Puppet 36

Chapter 2:
Summer 38

Cardboard Roll Flower Craft 40
Fruit Kebabs 42
Treasure Map 44
Sponge Balls 46
Crayon Art 48
Homemade Popsicles 50
Newspaper Art 52
Sock Caterpillar 54
Woven Magazine Mat 56
Painted Rocks 59
Food Coloring Tie-dye T-shirts 60
T-shirt Music Player Holder 62
Patio Paint 64
Coffee and Tea Stained
    Tank Top 66

Chapter 3:
Fall 68

Permanent Marker Mugs 70
Recycled Cereal Box File Holder 72
Greeting Card Bookmarks 74
Spooky Cardboard Rolls 76
Money Box 79
Halloween Silhouettes 80
Banana Ghosts, Clementine
    Pumpkins, and Apple Smiles 82
Backpack Tags 85
Eyeball Wreath 88
Ribbon Memo Board 90
Shoe-box Jewelry Box 92
T-shirt Key Chain 94

Chapter 4:
Winter 96

Snowman Handprints 98
No-sew Cinnamon Mats 100
3D Valentines 102
Juice Box Snowmen 104
Salt Dough 107
Candy Cane Chocolate Bark 110
Tissue Box Desk Organizer 112
Sock Arm Warmer 114
Sock Mug Warmer 116
Easy No-sew Hat 118
Gift in a Jar 120
Jar Lid Magnets 122
Paper Snowflakes 124

Templates 127
Index 128

Introduction

This book provides over 50 awesome activities to entertain young readers, using simple materials found around the home or classroom. There is a chapter of activities for each season of the year and within these you will find ideas for your favorite holidays such as Halloween, Christmas, Valentine's Day, Mother's Day, and Father's Day.

These seasonal activities provide engaging ways to keep kids busy, without the need for screens or batteries. Many of the activities within these pages can be used as decorations as well as gifts for loved ones. All of the activities are un-competitive and focus on children doing their personal best in each activity. Even better, many of the projects in this book help to promote recycling by suggesting ways that you can reuse and recycle household objects, making them inexpensive as well as kind

to the environment—look out for the green "eco-friendly" symbol throughout the book.

Guess What...

Each project has a Guess What? feature linked to it. These are provided for kids to "think outside the box" when they do an activity, giving them tidbits of history, geography, science, and more, which are connected to a specific part of the activity. This makes every Boredom Buster not only entertaining, but a bit educational, too (shhh … don't tell the kids!).

Learning Skills Developed by doing Boredom Busters

- *Reading (silently and out loud)*
- *Vocabulary development (what does "découpage" mean?)*
- *Math skills (using a ruler or measuring ingredients)*
- *Decision making (which activity will you do today?)*
- *Problem solving (I can't find the scissors!)*
- *Hand-eye coordination (pouring liquids or placing glue on an item)*

- *Concentration (paying attention to the activity)*
- *Patience (waiting for a result)*
- *Following directions (doing the steps of an activity in the right order)*
- *Creativity (blending colors)*
- *Gross motor skills (rolling or pressing)*
- *Fine motor skills (grasping a spoon or holding a paintbrush)*

At the start of each project you will find some key information. There is a guide to how long each activity takes as well as a Boredom Buster rating, explaining what you will get out of it. Finally, each project has an activity level rating, ranging from one to three stars—this will help you understand how simple (★) or how involved (★ ★ ★) an activity is.

BOREDOM BUSTERS TIPS

✓ *READ the whole project first before you start to DO the activity*

✓ *WASH YOUR HANDS before and after every activity*

✓ *PUT OUT the things that you will need for the activity before you start*

✓ *COVER your activity area with an activity mat or newspaper to avoid mess*

✓ *ROLL UP YOUR SLEEVES and put on an apron to protect your clothes*

✓ *DO ONE STEP AT A TIME and follow the instructions in order*

✓ *KEEP your activity and supplies safe and out of reach of young children. Small items can be choking dangers to young children*

✓ *WATCH for the stop sign symbol in activities. When you see it, it means stop and ask an adult for help*

✓ *DON'T RUSH an activity—be sure to take your time and enjoy the experience*

✓ *CLEAN UP after you do an activity*

✓ *BE POSITIVE and have fun doing these Boredom Busters!*

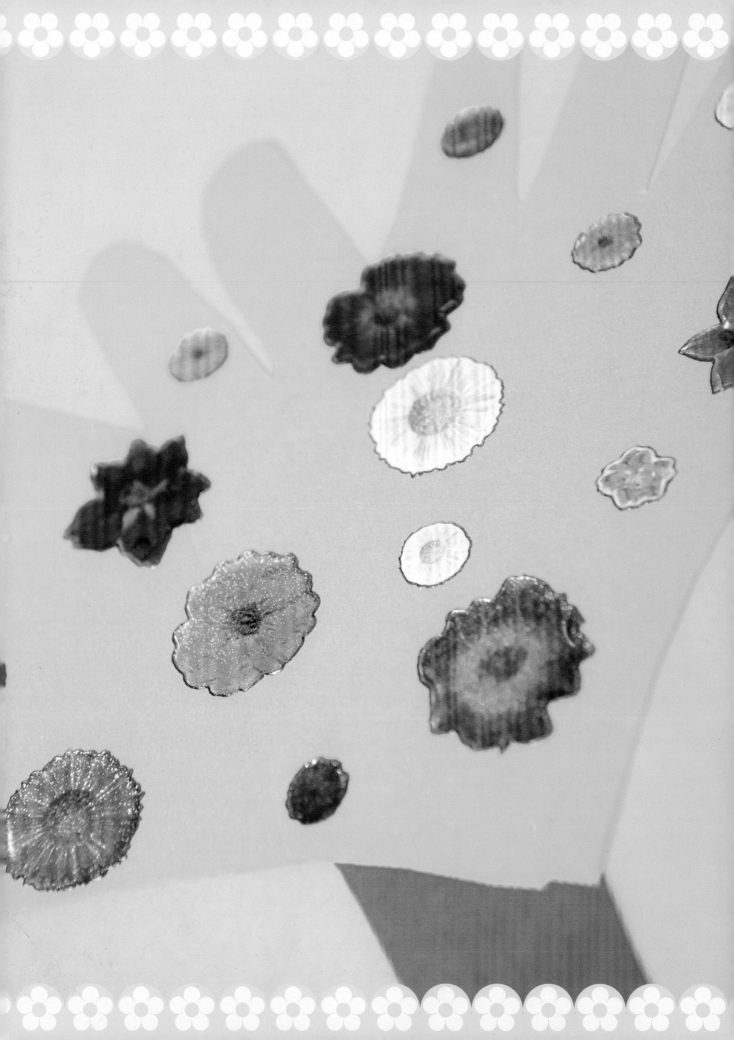

CHAPTER 1
SPRING

Washer Necklaces

A wearable Boredom Buster? Yes, please! These Washer Necklaces are fun to make (and they look AWESOME). A real one-of-a-kind piece of jewelry! They also make fantastic gifts, think: Mother's Day, teacher gifts, holidays, and more. Washer Necklaces are also a great and inexpensive birthday activity.

MAKE IT IN: **30 minutes**
BOREDOM BUSTER: **One time activity (but keeps forever)**
ACTIVITY LEVEL: ★

Things you need:

• Activity mat
• Flat metal washers in any size (available from hardware stores)
• Nail polish
• Paper towel
• Ribbon, yarn, or string
• Scissors

1 Place a flat metal washer on the activity mat to protect your surface. Using nail polish, paint one side of the washer.

2 You can paint it all one color or you can paint stripes or dots with different colors. You can paint splats. You can brush one color on, dab some of it off with a crumpled paper towel, and then paint another color on top of it, followed by dabbing it again with a crumpled paper towel.

3 Allow the painted washers to dry—this will take about five minutes. Once they are dry, turn them over and paint the other sides.

4 Cut a piece of ribbon, yarn, or string long enough to fit over your head when tied. Thread it through the center of the washer, tie a double knot at the ends, and wear your Washer Necklace with pride!

Guess What...
Nail Polish

In days long ago, the rich people of both China and Egypt used nail polish as a status symbol—to show off their wealth and power (poor people didn't wear nail polish). It is said the Egyptian Queen Nefertiti painted her nails red. The warriors of Babylon (who were men) painted their nails black. These days nail polish comes in a huge variety of colors from red, pink, purple, blue, and black to sparkly metallic gold and silver and glittery multicolor polish.

Paper Chain People

Making Paper Chain People is an easy Boredom Buster. By using different colored paper you can use them to decorate for any holiday. Try making a chain for a holiday card, birthday card, party invitation, or thank you card. You can switch up this activity by drawing legs for a male paper chain or a triangle skirt for a female paper chain.

MAKE IT IN: **15 minutes**
BOREDOM BUSTER: **One time activity (makes two paper chains)**
ACTIVITY LEVEL: ★ ★

Things you need:

• Construction paper or computer paper
• Scissors
• Pencil
• Marker pens, colored pencils, crayons, glitter glue, stickers

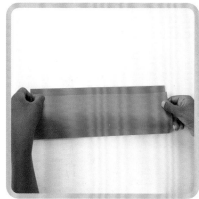

1 Fold paper in half vertically (long edge to long edge).

2 Open the paper out and use scissors to cut along the folded line.

3 Take one of the pieces of paper and fold it in half (short edge to short edge), and then in half again. Repeat with the second piece of paper. Press down firmly to make sharp creases along the folds.

Guess What... Paper

Paper is made out of wood pulp. To make paper you soak wood fiber in water, and then spread it onto a screen. Finally, you add a press on top to press out the water. The fiber bonds together and creates paper. The first known paper was made 2,000 years ago by the people of China from plant fibers.

4 Take one of the folded pieces of paper and draw a head at the top center of the paper. Draw a neck and then two arms extending past each side of the paper. Now draw the body and then two legs extending past each side of the paper. IMPORTANT: The arms and legs must extend past each side of the paper as this is what connects the Paper Chain People together.

5 Use scissors to carefully cut the person shape through all the paper layers. You can use your fingers to pull away the cut pieces of paper. Don't cut the folded arms or legs.

6 When the person is fully cut out, carefully unfold your paper chain people. Repeat steps 4–5 to make another chain out of the other piece of paper. Use sticky tape to join the two chains together at the arms and legs.

7 Decorate your Paper Chain People with marker pens, colored pencils, crayons, glitter glue, or stickers.

T-shirt Apron

Recycle an extra-large T-shirt into an apron! This fun, inexpensive, and no-sew activity is eco-friendly (giving new life to something meant for the trash bin). You can also decorate T-shirt Aprons and give them as a gift. And they aren't just for bakers—these aprons could be used for gardening, crafts, barbecues, and more!

Recycle a T-shirt for this project.

MAKE IT IN: **30 minutes**
BOREDOM BUSTER: **One time activity (you can use it again and again)**
ACTIVITY LEVEL: ★ ★ ★

Things you need:

- An extra-large adult size T-shirt
- Ruler
- Pencil
- Scissors
- Marker pens, fabric paint, fabric markers (optional)

1 Lay the T-shirt out on a flat surface. Using a ruler, measure and mark 2in (5cm) from either side of the neck collar.

2 Place your scissors just under the left armpit of the T-shirt and cut in a diagonal from the bottom of the armpit to the mark to the side of the collar. Turn your shirt around and repeat on the opposite side of the T-shirt, so you have removed both sleeves.

Guess What... Apron

The word apron comes from the French word *napperon*, which means a doily. Aprons can be made out of cloth, plastic, or leather. Aprons are not only worn to stop your clothing from getting dirty while cleaning; they are worn by blacksmiths, restaurant staff, barbers and hairdressers, bakers, artists, and woodworkers.

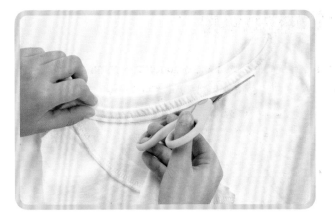

3 Flip the T-shirt over (so the front is facing down). Cut around the collar, through the top layer of fabric (the back of the T-shirt) only. Next, cut in a line from armpit to armpit, again cutting through the top layer of fabric (the back of the T-shirt) only. You will end up with a cutout of fabric—put it aside for future Boredom Busters such as the T-shirt Music Player Holder on page 62.

4 Then, turn your T-shirt around so that the bottom of the T-shirt is facing you. Cut the top layer of fabric (the back of the T-shirt) up along the right seam, ending the cut about 4in (10cm) from the armpit. Repeat on the other side of the T-shirt, cutting up the seam and ending about 4in (10cm) from the armpit.

5 Next, cut across the fabric, cutting from the 4in (10cm) mark on one side to the 4in (10cm) mark on the other side. You will have a rectangle of fabric, which you can put in your craft bin.

6 You should now have a 4in (10cm) band going across the back of your apron. On the left side, cut 2in (5cm) up along the left seam, then cut a line across the center of the band stopping just before you get to the seam on the other side. Then cut up 2in (5cm). This will create two fabric ties so you can tie your T-shirt Apron.

7 Put your head through the collar hole and tie your fabric band to check the size—you can trim the ties if you need to shorten them (or you can double knot them).

8 Decorate your T-shirt apron with marker pens or fabric paint, making sure to put cardboard between the layers of fabric so the colors don't bleed through the fabric.

Think of Me Tea Card

A Think of Me Tea Card is a great card to give for spring holidays (think: Mother's Day, Father's Day, teacher present, or grandparent's birthday). It combines an art project (making a card) with math (use shapes to draw the teacup). Switch it up by creating your own rhyming poem to go on the inside of the card. Something like: "Think of me when you drink this tea."

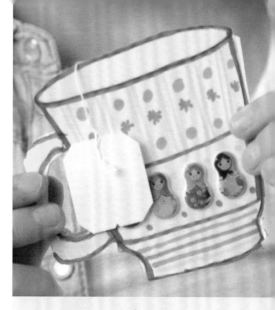

MAKE IT IN: **20 minutes**
BOREDOM BUSTER: **One time activity (but makes two cards)**
ACTIVITY LEVEL: ★

1 Fold your card or paper in half and use scissors to cut along the folded line. You will now have two half pages to make two cards with.

Things you need:

- Thin card or thick paper (construction paper works fine too)
- Pencil
- Scissors
- Marker pens, glitter glue, and stickers for decoration
- Tea bag (an individually wrapped one works best)
- Sticky tape

Guess What... Tea

Tea is made from the leaves of the tea plant, called *camellia sinensis*. Green tea and black tea are both made from the same tea plant. Tea is grown in Asia, Eastern Europe, Africa, and South America. The British first brought tea back from China to Europe in about 1600.

2 Fold one of the pieces in half and press down to make a tight fold. Now take your pencil and draw a teacup, making sure that the left side of the handle extends all the way to the fold line of the paper (this will create a folded card). To draw a teacup: using a pencil, start by drawing a thin oval. Then connect the two ends of the oval with a "U" shape. Then, on the side of the cup, draw the outline of half of a heart shape for the handle, starting at the top of the teacup and ending at the bottom.

3 When you are happy with the teacup shape, trace over it using a colored marker pen and then cut out the teacup, cutting through both layers of the card. Be sure not to cut through the folded edge on the left side of the card.

4 Decorate the front of the teacup card using marker pens, glitter glue, and/or stickers. Decorating ideas: try dots, flowers, stripes, lines, hearts, circles, or other patterns.

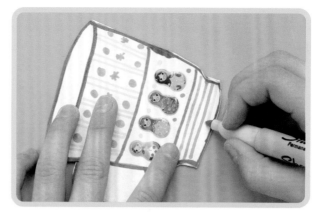

5 Open up your card and tape the tea bag to the left side of the card. If there is a string with your tea bag have it hang over the front of the card (use a piece of sticky tape to keep it in place). Write a message or poem on the inside of the card on the right—make sure you include the word "tea" in it!

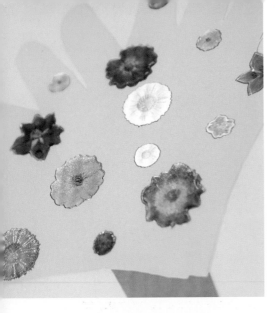

Handprint Tree

This Handprint Tree is easy, fun, and makes for a great present. It's also a terrific way to capture your handprint on paper. You can make one Handprint Tree with just your handprints. Or combine your handprints with those of your brother or sister and layer the "leaves" on top of each other for a sibling handprint tree.

MAKE IT IN: **20 minutes**
BOREDOM BUSTER: **One time activity (but it decorates for the whole season)**
ACTIVITY LEVEL: ★

Things you need:

- Activity mat or newspaper
- Construction paper in assorted colors (a background color plus green, brown, red, orange, and yellow)
- Pencil
- Scissors
- Glue stick
- Stickers: flowers, apples, or birds would all work well

1 Place your activity mat or newspaper on a flat surface and roll up your sleeves. Use a pencil to draw a tree trunk on brown construction paper.

2 Carefully cut out the tree trunk with scissors.

Guess What... Trees

There are more than 80,000 types of trees on the planet. Trees that keep their leaves all year round are called evergreen trees. Trees that lose their leaves in the winter are called deciduous trees. Some trees can live for hundreds of years.

3 Choose a color of construction paper for the leaves (green, red, orange, or yellow) and place it on your activity mat. Put your hand on the paper and trace round it—remember to spread out your fingers! Repeat with the other hand so that you have two handprints on the paper. Using scissors, cut out your handprints.

4 Choose a piece of colored construction paper for your background and start assembling your Handprint Tree on the paper: glue down the tree trunk first and then the handprints (with the fingers pointing out as the leaves).

5 Use stickers to decorate your tree— add as many as you want! You can even create little flowers next to the tree by drawing lines up from the bottom and putting a sticker at the top of each one.

Gym Bag Sock Buddies

These Gym Bag Sock Buddies are a Boredom Buster with a function! Have fun making these deodorizers and then bust bad smells when you use them in your gym bag—they will also fit inside shoes and boots! They will absorb the funky smells from your sports stuff overnight.

 Recycle a clean sock for this project.

MAKE IT IN: **20 minutes**
BOREDOM BUSTER: **One time activity (but you make and use them again and again)**
ACTIVITY LEVEL: ★

Things you need:

- Activity mat or newspaper
- Measuring cup
- 1 cup (200g) baking soda (bicarbonate of soda)
- 1 clean white sports sock
- 1 elastic band
- Permanent marker pens
- Spoon

NOTE: This makes one sock buddy; you'll need two if you're putting them in your trainers!

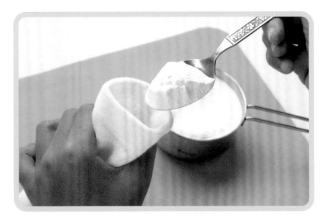

1 Lay your activity mat or newspaper out on a flat surface—this is to catch any baking soda (bicarbonate of soda) that spills. Measure out the baking soda and then pour it into the sock.

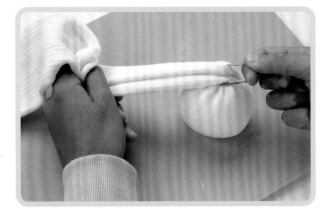

2 Knot the elastic band around the sock above the baking soda, creating a ball-like shape. Make sure you knot it well so that the baking soda does not spill out.

3 Use permanent marker pens to draw a face on the front of the sock ball. You could make a happy face, a funny face, and add features such as sunglasses or a mustache. Or you could draw an animal face, such as a bunny, owl, or puppy. It's your choice!

4 When you've finished drawing your face, your Gym Bag Sock Buddy is ready to be tucked in with your gym kit.

Guess What...
Baking Soda

Baking soda (which is called bicarbonate of soda in the UK) naturally absorbs strong odors. The scientific name for baking soda is sodium bicarbonate. It is non-toxic. Many people use an open box of baking soda in refrigerators to absorb odor from food. You can also sprinkle baking soda with water in plastic containers to get rid of food and drink smells. Baking soda is also widely used as an ingredient in baking cakes.

Spring Basket

Use this Spring Basket as a seasonal decoration, fill it with treats, or use it to collect objects. This activity is eco-friendly because it repurposes materials meant for the trash bin into something new. You could also switch up the colors and decorations and use this basket for other holidays, such as Halloween or Valentine's Day.

Recycle a plastic container for this project.

MAKE IT IN: 30 minutes
BOREDOM BUSTER: One time activity (but you can use it every year)
ACTIVITY LEVEL: ★★

Things you need:

- Activity mat or newspaper
- Double-sided tape (glue works fine too)
- Scissors
- 2-cup (500-ml) plastic container (recycle a clean plastic yogurt container)
- 8 x 15-in (20 x 38-cm) piece of felt (good colors for spring are green, blue, pink, purple)
- White school glue (PVA glue)
- Stickers, scrapbook supplies, fabric cutouts to decorate

1 Place your activity mat on a flat surface and roll up your sleeves. Cut six strips of double-sided tape, each one the height of the plastic container.

2 Place the double-sided tape, in vertical strips, around the plastic container.

3 Take the piece of felt and place your taped plastic container in the middle of your felt and wrap the fabric around, leaving a border of felt at the top and bottom.

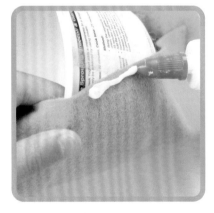

4 Place glue along one end of the felt and secure the other end in place.

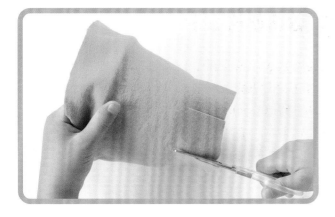

5 Using the scissors, cut wide slits from the bottom of the felt up to the base of the plastic container.

6 Place a line of glue around the bottom of the plastic container and press the bottom strips of fabric into the glue so that the felt will be secured to the bottom of the plastic container.

7 Now place a line of glue along the inside top of the plastic container and along the top of the felt. Fold the felt over the top edge and press it to the glue inside the plastic container.

8 Now it's time to decorate! Use stickers, scrapbook supplies, fabric cutouts, or make your own by cutting out shapes from felt.

Guess What...
Largest Basket

The largest basket ever made measured in at 72ft (22m) long, 48ft (14m) wide, and 40ft (12m) high and weighed just over 13 tonnes. This huge basket was made from wicker and bamboo in Saudi Arabia in 2010.

Découpage Tiles

Découpage Tiles is a great Boredom Buster to do after a vacation. Ideas for découpage materials: a map of where you went, an admission ticket, an image of something you saw, a picture of where you stayed, or a menu of what you ate. These Découpage Tiles make great decorations for your room or paperweights you can place on a table. And they are so, so easy!

Recycle a yogurt container for this project.

MAKE IT IN: **45 minutes**
BOREDOM BUSTER: **One time activity (but it decorates all season long)**
ACTIVITY LEVEL: ★ ★

Things you need:

- Activity mat
- Empty yogurt container
- White school glue (PVA glue)
- Water
- Ceramic tiles (inexpensive and available from building suppliers)
- Paintbrush
- Découpage materials: patterned paper, gift wrap, map, tickets, pictures, menu

1 Put your empty container on your activity mat. Pour one teaspoon of white glue and one teaspoon of water into the container. Stir well to mix together.

2 Place the ceramic tiles on the mat and, using a paintbrush, brush a thin layer of glue/water mixture all over the ceramic tile.

3 Next, prepare your découpage materials, cutting them into small pieces if necessary. Carefully place your découpage paper on top of the ceramic tile. Use your fingers to smooth out any air pockets.

Guess What...
Découpage

The word "découpage" comes from the French language and means "to cut out." Découpage is the art of decorating a surface with paper cutouts, which can be anything from colored paper cutouts to pictures from magazines. Each layer is coated with varnish until you end up with a smooth finish. Découpage is often used to decorate small items of furniture.

4 Apply another layer thin layer of glue/water mixture on top of paper, making sure you brush all the edges down. Let dry for about 30 minutes.

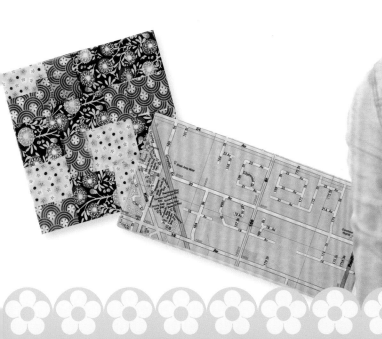

Potato Stamp Stationery

Making Potato Stamp Stationery is a fun Boredom Buster and makes for a lovely gift to give to parents, teachers, grandparents, and friends. Customize stationery (writing paper, cards, and envelopes) with designs and colors chosen by you. And this Potato Stamp Stationery is a must-do on your next vacation so you can send personalized letters to your friends.

MAKE IT IN: **60 minutes**
BOREDOM BUSTER: **One time activity (but you can make lots of stationery)**
ACTIVITY LEVEL: ★ ★ ★

Things you need:

- Apron
- Activity mat (or newspaper)
- Craft paint
- Paper plate
- Potato
- Cutting board
- Knife
- Cookie cutter
- White computer paper (or you could use blank cards or envelopes)

Stop for safety!
Ask an adult to help with cutting the potato.

1 Put on an apron, roll up your sleeves, and tie up your hair. Place your activity mat on a flat surface and pour some paint onto a paper plate.

2 Place your potato on a cutting board and carefully cut it in half, making sure that the cut surface is bigger than your cookie cutter.

Guess What...
Stationery

The word stationery refers to materials used for writing, such as paper, notecards, and envelopes, which were often matching. Personalized stationery often has a picture, name, or letter on it as a design. Banks, corporations, governments, and royal houses use custom stationery with their own unique logos and designs.

3 Press your chosen cookie cutter into the cut side of the potato. Ask an adult to help you cut around the edge of the cutter with a knife, then remove the cutter, leaving the raised shape on the potato. If you don't have cookie cutters, ask an adult to help you use a knife to cut out simple designs like a circle, square, diamond, or star.

4 Lay a piece of white computer paper on your activity mat. Dip the cookie cutter potato stamp into the paint.

5 Decide where you want your stamp—at the top of the page, in the center, across the top, a border down the left side, or a border all the way around the page. Take your potato stamp and press it firmly on the area of the paper where you want your potato stamp to appear. Lift the stamp straight up and off the paper to avoid smudging. Repeat your pattern along the paper, dipping the stamp in the paint again when you need more paint.

6 Potato Stamp Stationery ideas: allow your printed design to dry and then use the same stamp to print another color on top, this time offsetting the original design. Paint different areas of the stamp with different colors to make a rainbow effect. Stamp a repeating pattern of shapes (circle, diamond, circle, diamond).

Cotton Ball Sheep

What can you do with a Cotton Ball Sheep? Think: paperweight, desk decoration, or for role play. This Cotton Ball Sheep activity is eco-friendly as you can reuse a clean cup or container for the sheep's body. Easy to do on your own or with a group, you can make a whole herd or just one Cotton Ball Sheep.

Recycle a small plastic container for this project.

MAKE IT IN: 45 minutes
BOREDOM BUSTER: One time activity (but you can play with it again and again)
ACTIVITY LEVEL: ★★

Things you need:

- Activity mat or newspaper
- Paper or plastic cup (or recycle a clean, small yogurt container)
- White school glue (PVA glue)
- Cotton balls
- Black construction paper
- Scissors
- 2 styrofoam balls
- Black marker pen (googly eyes will work fine too)

1 Place your activity mat or newspaper on a flat surface and roll up your sleeves. Place your cup or yogurt container on the mat and apply a line of glue around the top of the cup.

2 One by one, place cotton balls along the glue line around the cup.

3 Continue adding lines of glue and cotton balls around the cup until the entire cup (including the top) is covered in cotton balls.

4 Next, take your black construction paper and cut a medium-sized oval shape for the sheep's face and two small oval shapes for the sheep's ears.

5 Take the two styrofoam balls and using a black marker pen, draw a small circle in the center of each of the balls. Glue these "eyes" onto the sheep's face.

Guess What... Sheep

Male sheep are called rams. Female sheep are called ewes. Sheep are found on every continent on Earth except for Antarctica. There are over 200 different kinds of sheep. An adult sheep can weigh anywhere between 80–400lbs (35–189kg).

6 Glue the sheep's face onto the Cotton Ball Sheep. Glue the small ovals (sheep's ears) onto either side of the sheep's face.

Homemade Bird Feeder

This Homemade Bird Feeder Boredom Buster is easy to make. Not only will it decorate your trees but it will also attract birds (which you can watch from your window). This activity is eco-friendly as it recycles cardboard toilet roll tubes.

Recycle a cardboard toilet paper roll for this project.

MAKE IT IN: **20 minutes**
BOREDOM BUSTER: **One time activity (but you can use it over and over again)**
ACTIVITY LEVEL: ★

Things you need:

- Birdseed (a mixture of seeds such as sunflower or pumpkin work fine too)
- 2 plates
- Peanut butter (or nut-free spread)
- Tablespoon
- Toilet roll tube
- String
- Scissors

1 Pour the birdseed onto a plate—you'll need about three tablespoons to make one bird feeder.

2 Put a tablespoon of peanut butter or nut-free spread onto another plate. Take your toilet roll tube and use the back of the spoon to cover it with the peanut butter or nut-free spread. NOTE: This can get a bit messy! Add more peanut butter if needed to make sure all of the toilet roll tube is covered.

3 Hold the toilet roll tube by the ends and place it in the plate of birdseed. Gently roll it back and forth so that the birdseed sticks to the peanut butter. Make sure you cover the entire toilet roll tube in birdseed.

4 Cut a length of string approximately 12in (30cm) long. Thread the yarn through the toilet roll tube and tie a double knot at the ends to secure it. Now you are ready to go outside and hang your Homemade Bird Feeder to a branch.

Guess What...
Sunflower Seeds

The seeds that attract the biggest collection of birds are sunflower seeds. Sunflowers are large plants that turn their flowers during the day from east to west to follow the sun. Sunflower seeds come from the dark center part of the sunflower. The sunflower petals can be made into a dye. We use sunflower oil in cooking. Sunflower seeds have a hard black shell. You can buy sunflower seeds with or without the shell.

Sock Monsters

This is a great way to reuse socks left in the bottom of the laundry basket. You know the ones... the-other-matching-sock-is-missing socks. Give these old socks new life by turning them into Sock Monsters. These are great to make and pack perfectly for a Boredom Buster on the go.

Repurpose a clean sock for this project.

MAKE IT IN: **30 minutes**
BOREDOM BUSTER: **One time activity (but you'll want to make it again)**
ACTIVITY LEVEL: ★★

Things you need:

- Clean sock
- Marker pen
- Felt (any color)
- Scissors
- 2 buttons
- Needle
- Sewing thread
- White school glue (PVA glue)
- Yarn
- Ribbon (optional)

1 Put your hand inside the sock so that your fingertips are at the tip of the toe portion of the sock. Using a marker pen, mark dots where you would like to place eyes and mouth and then remove your hand from the sock.

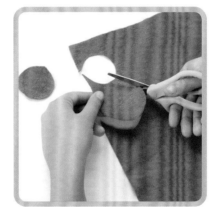

2 Cut out two circles of felt. You can either cut the circles freehand or draw around something round, like a button.

3 Glue the felt circles where you marked the eyes. Allow to dry and then sew a button on top of each circle of felt.

Guess What... Monsters

We all know monsters are not real. However, there are many legends around the world about monsters. In Scotland, people tell stories about the myth of the Loch Ness Monster—a lake creature. In North America, people tell stories about a Sasquatch (also known as Bigfoot or Yeti)—an ape-like creature who lives in forests.

4 Using a marker pen, draw a "U" shape on a piece of felt. Draw a line to connect the "U" at the top and then cut out this shape (this will be the Sock Monster mouth). Place a dab of glue where you marked the mouth position on the sock and stick the mouth in place.

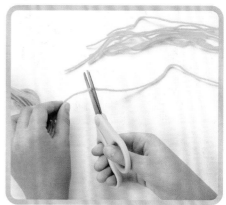

5 Cut strips of yarn for hair—it can be whatever length you choose. Gather all the strips together and tie a knot in the middle of them.

6 Put your hand inside the sock to have a look at your Sock Monster and decide where to position the hair. Place a dab of glue on the top of the head and press the knot in the yarn firmly in place. Use scissors to trim the hair if desired.

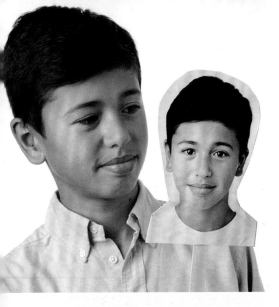

Family Photo Puppet

Family Photo Puppets are brilliant Boredom Busters. They are also easy to pop in your backpack for fun on the go while you travel. Photo puppets don't have to be just family photos: you could use pictures of your friends, your teachers or sports coach, favorite stars—even cartoon characters. This is a great role play activity to do at home, in the classroom, or on vacation.

MAKE IT IN: **15 minutes**
BOREDOM BUSTER: **One time activity (but you can role play over and over)**
ACTIVITY LEVEL: ★ ★

Things you need:

- Photographs or pictures
- Cereal box cardboard if your photo isn't printed on heavy paper (optional)
- White school glue (PVA glue)
- Scissors
- Popsicle sticks (available from craft stores)

1 Choose some family photos that you would like to make into puppets. Here we've used a photo of just the head, but you could use photos that show the whole head and body, too.

2 If the photo paper is thin (for example, if you printed the photo onto computer paper), glue the photo onto a piece of cereal box cardboard.

Think about other Photo Puppets you can make using photos from magazines. Princesses? Pirates? Animals? Superheroes? Then try making up stories using your Photo Puppets.

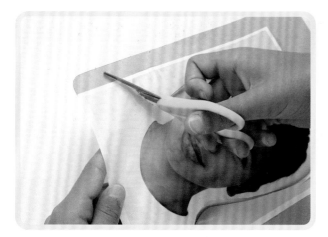

3 Using scissors, cut around the photo so that you cut out the background and just keep the figure of the family member.

Guess What...
Muppets

Jim Henson, a puppeteer from the United States of America, created the world famous Muppets. He made up the word "Muppets" from the word marionette (a puppet controlled by strings) and puppet. Muppets are made out of rubber, plastic, and fabric. Famous Muppets include Kermit the Frog, Miss Piggy, and Oscar the Grouch.

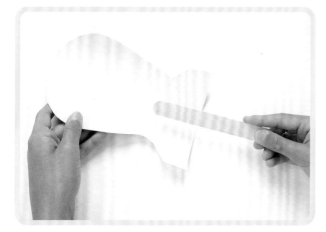

4 Take one popsicle stick and place a line of glue at the top of the stick. Gently place the photo onto the glue. Press firmly so that it sticks in place. Allow to dry for 2–3 minutes. Then start making up stories and adventures with your Family Photo Puppets!

CHAPTER 2
SUMMER

Cardboard Roll Flower Craft

This Cardboard Roll Flower Craft is easy, inexpensive, and encourages recycling. Thread through some pipe cleaner, ribbon, or string, and it becomes a hanging decoration. Glue it onto a journal, scrapbook page, or card and it becomes a 3D decoration. Make a bunch and glue them side by side and you have a fantastic wall decoration.

Recycle a cardboard toilet paper roll.

MAKE IT IN: **20 minutes**
BOREDOM BUSTER: **One time activity (but keeps forever)**
ACTIVITY LEVEL: ★ ★

Things you need:

- Toilet roll tubes
- Scissors
- Activity mat
- White school glue (PVA glue)
- Craft paint
- Paintbrush
- Ribbon or string for hanging (optional)

1 Cut your toilet roll tube into five equal parts, each one about 1 in (2.5cm) wide. As you cut the tube may get squished from a circle shape to an oval shape due to the pressure of cutting and holding—this is fine because you want an oval shape. If the toilet roll parts are not quite oval enough, give them a gentle pull at each end to stretch them into an oval shape.

2 Now arrange your ovals into a flower shape on an activity mat. The ends of the ovals should be touching at the center.

Use these to decorate your bedroom, classroom, or even a party table!

3 Pick up the bottom oval and apply glue to the outside bottom edges. Stick this to the two ovals either side and then repeat with the two ovals at the top until they are all connected and you have a five-petal flower.

4 Gently squeeze the glued edges together and hold for a few seconds. Allow to dry completely (this will take about 10 minutes).

5 When your flowers are dry, use a paintbrush and some paint to carefully paint the edges of the flower. If you would like to hang your flowers as decorations, thread a piece of narrow ribbon or string through one of the petals and tie in a knot.

Guess What...
Toilet Paper

It seems that toilet paper was first used in China around 851 AD. However, the idea of toilet paper didn't catch on right away. What was used instead of toilet paper, you might wonder? The Romans used a sponge on a stick. English upper class used pages from books. The Inuit (people of the Canadian Arctic) used snow. People from the Middle Ages used straw—ouch!

Fruit Kebabs

Making Fruit Kebabs is a great way to have fun with your food! This rainbow of fruit on a stick is easy to make. It is also a healthy choice for an after-school snack and a crowd-pleasing party food. Younger kids (who shouldn't handle sharp edges) should use wooden popsicle sticks instead of wooden skewers.

MAKE IT IN: **20 minutes**
BOREDOM BUSTER: **One time activity (but you can make them again and again)**
ACTIVITY LEVEL: ★ ★

Stop for safety!
Be careful of the pointy tip of wooden skewers.

1 Wash your hands (always do this before handling food), roll up your sleeves, and put on an apron.

Things you need:

- Apron
- Cutting board
- Knife
- Slices of pineapple and melon
- Selection of washed fruit (strawberries, purple grapes, blueberries)
- Cookie cutters (star and heart shapes work well)
- Wooden skewers or popsicle sticks (popsicle sticks are available from craft stores)
- Serving plate or cup

2 Take the melon and pineapple slices and place them on your cutting board. Gently press cookie cutters into the melon and pineapple to create fruit shapes. Put the fruit shapes to the side.

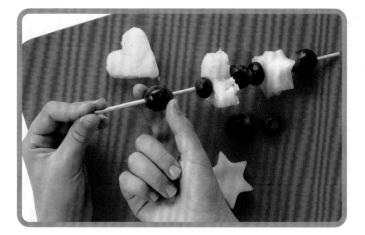

3 Now start threading pieces of fruit, one after the other, onto your sticks. You could use this order: melon, strawberries, pineapple, purple grapes, blueberries, or switch it up and create your own arrangement. You could do a fruit kebab all of one kind of fruit. You could do a fruit kebab of the same family of fruit (like different types of melons), or all in the same color. NOTE: If you are using a wooden popsicle stick you can't add blueberries or grapes as they won't stay on. However, melon, strawberries, and pineapple work brilliantly!

4 Arrange the finished Fruit Kebabs on their sides on a serving plate or stand them up in a cup.

Tip

You can make your fruit kebabs on the morning of a party. Simply make them up, place on a serving tray, cover with plastic wrap (cling film), and refrigerate until ready to serve.

Guess What...
Melons

Melons grow in warm areas of the world. They are annual plants, meaning they last just one season and then the seeds have to be replanted for the next growing season. Popular kinds of melon include: cantaloupe, honeydew, and casaba. Watermelons are actually considered part of the gourd family—like pumpkins!

Treasure Map

Making a Treasure Map can be an activity today—and a game tomorrow! Tracking down locations on a Treasure Map is a fun indoor activity for a rainy day or an entertaining outdoor scavenger hunt on a sunny day. This Boredom Buster makes a tea-stained Treasure Map, but you could use the same method to make ancient-looking paper for invitations and party posters.

MAKE IT IN: **24 hours**
BOREDOM BUSTER: **One time activity (but you'll want to make it again)**
ACTIVITY LEVEL: ★

1 Ask an adult to help you boil a kettle full of water. Put the tea bags in the teapot.

2 While you wait for the water to boil, scrunch up a sheet of white paper. Unscrunch the paper and lay it out flat in the baking tray.

Things you need:

- Kettle
- 4 tea bags (black tea)
- Teapot
- White computer paper
- Rectangular baking tray (with sides)
- Spoon
- Wire cooling rack
- Paper towel
- Marker pens, stickers, and glitter glue

Guess What...
Buried Treasure

The largest amount of Anglo-Saxon gold was discovered, by surprise, in 2009 in Staffordshire, U.K. Terry Herbert found over 650 gold objects and 530 silver objects by using a metal detector over some farmland owned by his friend. The buried treasure is very valuable in terms of money and historical value. No one knows who buried the treasure.

Stop for safety!
Ask an adult to help with boiling and pouring the hot water.

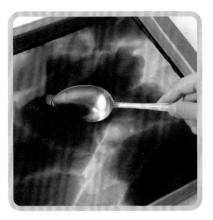

3 When the kettle has boiled, carefully pour the water into the teapot (ask an adult for help) and leave it to "brew" for 10 minutes. Then pour the tea into the baking tray, being sure to completely cover the white crumpled paper.

4 Use a spoon to poke down any parts of the paper that might not be covered and then leave the paper to sit in the tea for 1–2 hours (depending on how brown you would like it).

5 Place some sheets of paper towel under the wire rack to mop up any drips. Carefully take the paper out of the tea. It will be delicate so be careful not to rip it. A tear or two might make it look old but a big rip might break it in two. Lay the tea-stained paper on the wire rack and let dry overnight.

6 Decorate your treasure map with marker pens, stickers, or glitter glue. Be sure to draw a compass showing North, South, East, and West, along with trees, footsteps, and paths. And, of course, don't forget to draw an "X" to mark the spot where the treasure is to be found!

Sponge Balls

Playing with Sponge Balls is a fun summer water activity and they can be used over and over again. And with no sharp edges you can use these sponge balls for a game of water tag or as an alternative to water balloons. You can also use them for scrubbing and washing, too!

MAKE IT IN: **20 minutes**
BOREDOM BUSTER: **One time activity (but you'll want to make it again)**
ACTIVITY LEVEL: ★★

Things you need:

- 3 new, clean, rectangular sponges in assorted colors
- Ruler
- Marker pen
- Scissors
- Elastic cord or elastic band

1 Take one of the sponges and measure and mark it vertically into three equal sections, using a ruler and marker pen (you could also just estimate the three equal sections by eye). Repeat for the other two sponges.

2 Using scissors, cut along the lines to make nine sponge strips.

3 Put the sponges back together, this time mixing up the colors. Layer the strips on top of each other so that you have three strips across and three strips down.

4 Take a length of elastic cord and tie it around the middle of all the sponge strips to attach them together. Tie a double knot to secure and trim the ends of the cord. You could also use an elastic band instead of cord, and loop it two or three times around the middle of the strips.

5 Gently pull up the ends of the sponge strips to form them into a sponge ball.

Guess What... Sponges

Household sponges are manufactured using man-made materials but did you know there is an animal called a sponge? There are 5,000 species of sponge that live in water (usually oceans). While sponges eat food they are unlike other animals as they do not have body parts or move around. Sponges are found attached, underwater, to rocks or coral reefs.

Crayon Art

Crayon Art creates an impressive rainbow of color. It is part art project and part science project—why do you think the crayons melt? The results are fantastic! This is a great outside activity in the summer, because you can make your Crayon Art leaning up against a fence or a wall so your canvas can stand up. You can use any size canvas; you just need enough crayons to cover the width of it.

Reuse old crayons for this project.

MAKE IT IN: 2 hours
BOREDOM BUSTER: One time activity (but you'll want to make it again)
ACTIVITY LEVEL: ★ ★ ★

Things you need:

- Newspaper
- 17 crayons (new or used—just make sure they are all the same length)
- 6 x 8-in (15 x 20-cm) piece of art canvas
- White school glue (PVA glue)
- Sticky tape
- Apron
- Extension lead (optional)
- Hairdryer

1 Lay some newspaper out on a flat surface. Choose 17 crayons; you can either unwrap the crayon paper or keep the crayons with their labels on.

Stop for safety!
Remember—melted crayon wax is HOT so do not touch the melting colors.

2 Arrange the crayons along the top of the canvas so that they are all pointing downward. Move them around a bit to get the color layout that you like best.

3 Remove the crayons from the canvas, making sure you can remember the order that you liked. Apply two or three lines of glue across the top of the canvas and stick the crayons in place tightly next to each other. Allow to dry for about five minutes before moving the canvas.

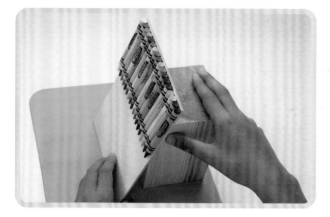

4 When the glue has dried and the crayons are fixed to the canvas, lean your canvas up against something. It's best if you can do this outside—for example, next to a wall or fence—but it's fine if you do it inside, too. Either way, you need to place some more newspaper or an activity mat at the bottom of the canvas—this will catch any drops of wax as they melt. (You might want to tape the newspaper to the wall or fence to secure it in place.) Put on an apron to protect your clothes.

Guess What...
Crayons

Coloring crayons (also called wax crayons) are made of waxes like paraffin wax, beeswax, and carnauba wax. To make coloring crayons, wax is melted and mixed with dry color and then set in molds to create crayon shapes. Coloring crayons are sold all over the world.

5 Plug in your hairdryer (using an extension lead if you're doing this outside), and turn it on to its lowest setting. Point the hairdryer downward so the crayon wax drips down and onto the ends of the crayons. Gently move the hairdryer back and forth, over 2–3 crayons at a time. The crayons will start to melt within a few minutes.

6 Continue blowing hot air onto 2–3 crayons at a time until the crayons have melted down the canvas. It's up to you to decide how much "crayon melt" you want! Turn the hairdryer off and unplug it. Leave the canvas standing up on the newspaper until the crayon wax is cool (about one hour).

Homemade Popsicles

MAKE IT IN: **12 hours (overnight is best)**

BOREDOM BUSTER: **One time activity (but you'll want to make it again)**

ACTIVITY LEVEL: ★ ★

Homemade Popsicles are a delightful and delicious treat on a hot day. And they can be made with ingredients you already have in your kitchen pantry. These no-cook treats are easy to prepare, freeze, and enjoy. You can make single flavor Homemade Popsicles or layer them (as shown in this Boredom Buster). They are great for summer parties.

Things you need:

- 2 large bowls
- 1 packet of instant chocolate pudding (Jello Instant Pudding or Angel Delight)
- 1 packet of instant vanilla pudding (Jello Instant Pudding or Angel Delight)
- Milk
- Whisk
- Popsicle molds
- Tablespoon
- Cookie crumbs, chocolate chips, cut fruit such as strawberries, blueberries, raspberries (optional)

1 In a large bowl, prepare the instant chocolate pudding with the milk, according to the directions on the packaging. Make up the instant vanilla pudding in the second bowl in the same way.

2 Place your popsicle molds on a flat surface and use spoon two tablespoons of instant chocolate pudding into each popsicle mold.

Guess What... Pudding

In Britain, pudding is used to describe sweet desserts. They are generally soft, thick, and spongy in texture. Common puddings in Britain can be boiled or steamed and made of ingredients such as dried fruits, spices, breadcrumbs, and candied fruit peels. In North America, pudding is a cold creamy, custard-like treat most often made of milk. North American puddings come in various flavors like chocolate, vanilla, and lemon.

3 Spoon two tablespoons of instant vanilla pudding into each popsicle mold, on top of the chocolate. If you want to add any extras such as cookie crumbs, chocolate chips, or cut fruit, add a layer between the pudding layers. Continue layering chocolate and vanilla pudding until the mixture is about ½in (1cm) away from the top of your container. Add the tops of the popsicle molds.

4 When all your popsicle molds are filled with the layered pudding mixture, place them in the freezer until frozen—this will take several hours, so it's best to make them the night before you want to eat them.

If you don't have popsicle molds you can layer the puddings into paper cups arranged on a cookie (baking) sheet. Place in the freezer for 30 minutes, then remove and insert a popsicle stick into the center of each one. Place a small square of plastic wrap (cling film) over the popsicle, making a hole in the center so the popsicle stick pokes through, and return to the freezer until frozen.

Newspaper Art

This Boredom Buster is an eco-friendly activity as it reuses old newspaper and other materials into a piece of art, such as a beautiful beach scene. Use a section of newspaper that has lots of text—pictures or large headings won't work here. Look for different colors and textures in things you can use that would normally be recycled—colored plastic bags, brown envelopes, or corrugated card.

Reuse newspaper for this project.

MAKE IT IN: **30 minutes**
BOREDOM BUSTER: **One time activity (but you'll want to make it again)**
ACTIVITY LEVEL: ★★

Things you need:

- White computer paper
- Pencil
- Scissors
- Newspaper
- Small container (recycle a clean yogurt container)
- White school glue (PVA glue)
- Paintbrush
- Canvas board
- Plastic bags
- A brown paper bag, envelope, or piece of corrugated card
- Aluminum foil

1 Take a piece of white computer paper and draw silhouettes of the palm tree trunk and a circle, using the photograph as a guide. When you are happy with your silhouettes, cut them out with scissors.

2 Place the tree trunk silhouette on your newspaper page, making sure you choose a section that has solid text with no pictures or advertisements. Using a pencil, trace around your silhouette and then cut it out.

3 Mix a small amount of glue (about one teaspoon) with the same amount of water in a small container or clean yogurt pot. Stir well to mix, and then use a paintbrush to paint glue on the back of your newspaper silhouette.

4 Gently place your newspaper silhouette to the right of your canvas. Brush some of the glue mixture on top of the newspaper silhouette to seal it (it will dry clear). Allow the glue to dry.

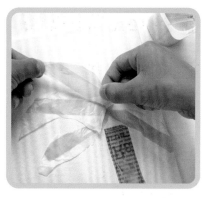

5 Now cut out some palm tree leaves from the plastic bag. Palm tree leaves are like the shape of a banana. Use a small amount of glue to stick them to the paper. You don't need to paint the glue over the top.

Guess What...
Newspapers

By the late 1900s, Europe had over 2,600 daily newspapers and North America had over 2,200. People read newspapers for information on topics such as international and national events, local news, weather, sports, entertainment, careers, and more. The invention of computers greatly changed the newspaper business because people could read news online instead of on paper.

6 Cut out a long rectangle of brown paper bag, envelope, or card, and glue it along the bottom of the paper to make a strip of sand.

7 Use the circle template you made in step 1 to cut out a sun from foil and stick it in the top corner of the paper. You can also add additional shapes cut from newspaper as in steps 1–4.

Sock Caterpillar

This no-sew Sock Caterpillar is easy to make. Take an old, clean sock (perhaps one that has lost its partner in the laundry?) and turn it into a fun Boredom Buster. This Sock Caterpillar makes a great art project, decoration, and role play figure. Who knew you could bust boredom with a sock?

Repurpose a clean sock for this project.

MAKE IT IN: **20 minutes**
BOREDOM BUSTER: **One
   time activity (but you'll
   want to make it again)**
ACTIVITY LEVEL: ★ ★

Things you need:

- 1 clean sock
- Cotton balls (paper towel, tissue, or toilet paper would work fine, too)
- 4 or 5 elastic hairbands
- Styrofoam ball and marker pen (or you can use googly eyes)
- White school glue (PVA glue)
- Pipe cleaner
- Scissors

1 Fill the sock with cotton balls, making sure you push them down to the end.

2 Place one elastic band over the end of the sock and twist it in place to prevent the cotton balls from moving about. This will form the caterpillar's head. Take another 3 or 4 hairbands and tie them around the sock at regular intervals to make the sections of the body.

3 Now take your two Styrofoam balls and use a marker pen to draw on the eyes.

4 Place two blobs of glue on the first section (the caterpillar's head) and glue the eyeballs in place.

5 Cut the pipe cleaner into two lengths. Place two dots of glue on top of the caterpillar's head, stick the pipe cleaners in place, and curl the ends to make antennae. Done!

Guess What... Caterpillars

The word caterpillar comes from the Latin *catta pilosa*, which means "hairy cat." Some caterpillars are hairy and some have bare skin. Caterpillars are the larvae of butterflies and moths. Some caterpillars stay in caterpillar form for days and others for years before they change into a butterfly or moth—this is known as *metamorphosis*.

Woven Magazine Mat

Making a Magazine Mat is a fun activity that encourages repurposing and recycling. Everyone has old magazines about so finding the supplies for this Boredom Buster is easy!

Recycle a magazine that you've finished reading.

MAKE IT IN: **60 minutes**

BOREDOM BUSTER: **One time activity (but you can use it over and over again)**

ACTIVITY LEVEL: ★ ★ ★

Things you need:

• Old magazines
• Clear packing tape
• Activity mat
• Scissors

1 Cleanly tear 20 pages from a magazine. You could tear a mishmash of print and graphic pages. You could also choose to have a rainbow of colors in the pages, or just choose pages with one main color (so if the main color on the page is blue, then the main color in the Woven Magazine Mat will be blue).

2 Next, organize the torn pages into two groups of 10 pages each. Take one group of pages and start folding them on your activity mat—each one will be folded three times. Turn the first page so the long edge is along the bottom and fold it upward in half.

One Magazine Mat can be hung as art or used as a place mat. Two mats taped together can be a desk mat. Three mats taped together can be a table runner. Five mats taped together can be a square basket. This Woven Magazine Mat can turn into so many Boredom Busters!

3 Press along the crease with your finger.

4 Now fold the page upward in half again and press the crease down with your finger. Repeat the folding and creasing one more time so that you have a long narrow strip about the width of your thumb.

Guess What... Weaving

When you cross over and under two separate materials, you are weaving. Many cultures are famous for their weaving: the people of Ancient China were known for silk weaving, The Maya (people of Mexico and Central America) were known for weaving cotton, and the Navajo (North American Indians) were known for weaving colorful wool blankets.

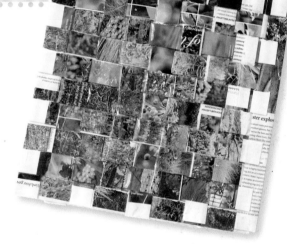

5 Keeping the magazine pages in your two groups, repeat this folding with all the pages of torn paper to create 20 magazine strips.

6 Next, take one magazine strip and lay it sideways in front of you. This will be the bottom border of the mat. Then, take nine magazine strips and position them, pointing up, over and under the bottom border.

IMPORTANT: Use a strip of clear packing tape to tape the bottom border and nine border strips down onto the activity mat. This is important because the paper will move around while you are weaving and taping them down and together will make weaving much easier. You won't be able to remove the packing tape once it is stuck down, so carefully tape it in place the first time.

7 Next, take the second group of magazine strips and start weaving them one at a time through the taped-down magazine strips. Each strip should go over and under, over and under, until it is in position. The paper might move around a bit—just be patient and continue weaving. Push each strip down toward the bottom of the mat before you start weaving the next one, to keep them tightly woven together.

8 Once all the magazine strips are woven and pushed together, making a tight weave, cut a strip of clear packing tape the length of your Woven Magazine Mat. Place the strip of tape next to the packing tape covering the bottom border. Continue placing strips of clear packing tape to cover the entire mat. The packing tape keeps the weave together and also protects the mat.

9 Turn your Woven Magazine Mat over and cover the other side with clear packing tape. Use scissors to trim off any extra bits of tape.

Painted Rocks

Painted Rocks are a classic Boredom Buster. Go for a walk on the beach or in the woods and pick up different sized rocks. Bring them home, give them a wash in water, and get the paint out to decorate them. A great activity at home, in the classroom, or on vacation!

MAKE IT IN: **45 minutes**
BOREDOM BUSTER: **One time activity (but you can use it again and again)**
ACTIVITY LEVEL: ★

Things you need:

- Apron
- Activity mat (or newspaper)
- Clean, dry rocks
- Craft paint—you could use Patio Paint (see page 64) for this activity
- Cardboard egg carton
- Paintbrushes
- Water and small plastic container (to clean brushes)
- White school glue (PVA glue)
- Googly eyes (available from craft stores)

1 Put on an apron, roll up your sleeves, and tie up your hair. Put your rocks on your activity mat and pour some craft paint into your cardboard egg carton sections.

2 Paint your rocks. You can paint the rocks individual colors or experiment with different color patters like lines, dots, swirls, zigzags, colored sections, or even a rainbow effect! Allow the paint to dry.

3 When the paint is dry, place a dab of glue where you would like your eyes to be and add a googly eye—or two or three!

Guess What... Rock Art

Ancient and prehistoric drawings, paintings, and carvings on stones are called rock art. Rock art often shows people, handprints, and animals. Rock art can tell stories of human life and traditions. In 2012, rock art that is believed to date back 20,000 years was discovered in Australia!

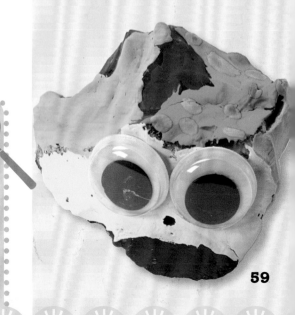

59

Food Coloring Tie-dye T-shirts

Recycle a shampoo bottle container for this project.

MAKE IT IN: **24 hours**
BOREDOM BUSTER: **One time activity (but you'll want to make it again)**
ACTIVITY LEVEL: ★ ★

Things you need:

- Apron
- Activity mat (or newspaper)
- White cotton T-shirt
- Large plastic bowl
- ½ cup (125ml) white vinegar
- Water
- Elastic bands
- Small squirt bottle (you could recycle a clean shampoo bottle)
- Food coloring in different colors
- Rubber gloves (optional: you don't have to wear them, but you may get food coloring on your fingers if not)
- Resealable plastic bag
- ½ cup (120g) salt

Get outside to make these tie-dye T-shirts! Reuse a favorite cotton T-shirt or use a new one. Wash Food Coloring Tie-dye T-shirts separately from other clothes for the first three washes, as some of the dye may run into your other clothes.

1 Roll up your sleeves, tie up your hair, and put on an apron (food coloring stains clothes, so you need to protect your clothing). Place your activity mat on a flat surface. Put your T-shirt into a large plastic bowl and pour over the vinegar and ½ cup (125ml) water—this helps prepare the fabric for the dye. Leave to soak for about 30 minutes.

2 Lift the T-shirt out of the bowl and squeeze it to wring it out. Roll the T-shirt into a long sausage shape and then tie three or four elastic bands around the fabric, spacing them however you like. You could pinch it together in the middle and secure with an elastic band to create a spiral design, or tie knots in the T-shirt for yet another tie-dye design.

3 Fill the squirt bottle with ½ cup (125ml) water and add eight drops of food coloring. Put the cap on the bottle and shake to mix well.

4 Place your T-shirt on your activity mat and put on a pair of rubber gloves. Squirt the food coloring mixture onto one area of the T-shirt, then turn it over and squirt the rest of the color mixture onto the other side.

5 Repeat steps 3 and 4 with your other food coloring colors, mixing up the colors in the squirt bottle and staining a different area of the T-shirt each time.

6 When your T-shirt is completely soaked in food coloring and water, place the T-shirt roll into a resealable plastic bag and leave to rest in the bag overnight.

7 The next day, take the T-shirt out of the bag and remove the elastic bands. Pour the salt and ½ cup (125ml) of water into a large bowl. Plunge the T-shirt into the salt water to set the dye and then wring the T-shirt out.

8 Rinse your dyed T-shirt in clean water several times until the water runs clear—take care when you rinse, as splashes of water may stain you and your clothes as the food coloring rinses off. Wring it out a final time and hang out to dry—preferably in the sun.

Guess What... Tie-dye

Tie-dye is the term for the process of twisting, knotting, and crumpling fabric, binding it with string or elastics, and applying dye to the fabric. In the 1960s many popular musicians, such as the legendary Jimi Hendrix, wore tie-dye shirts.

T-shirt Music Player Holder

Making a T-shirt Music Player Holder is a fun and functional activity. It is eco-friendly because it recycles an old, worn T-shirt. This is a great activity to do (and take!) on vacation or to do at home. It could also come in handy for carrying small things like crayons, cards, tickets, and more.

Recycle an old T-shirt for this project.

MAKE IT IN: 30 minutes
BOREDOM BUSTER: One time activity (but you'll want to make it again)
ACTIVITY LEVEL: ★

Things you need:

- Activity mat
- An old, worn T-shirt sleeve and some strips of T-shirt fabric (reuse from the T-shirt Apron on page 14!)
- Scissors
- Strong glue
- Clothespins
- Fabric paint to decorate (optional)

1 Place your activity mat on a flat surface and roll up your sleeves. Position the T-shirt sleeve on your mat. Using scissors, cut off any frayed edges so that you have a straight line and your sleeve is more like a rectangle shape.

2 Position the sleeve so that the edge you have just trimmed is at the bottom. Apply a line of glue along both inside edges and press the two layers of fabric together. Use a couple of clothespins to pin the fabric together securely. Wait for the glue to dry—this should take about 10 minutes.

3 Using fabric paint, decorate one or both sides of the T-shirt Music Player Holder.

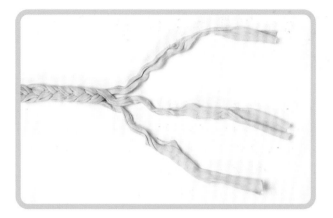

4 Take three long strips of T-shirt fabric and place them on your activity mat. Each strip needs to be about 2in (5cm) wide. Knot them together at one end and start braiding. To do this, move the strip at the right over the strip in the middle, then move the strip at the left over the strip in the middle—keep going. You can either make a shoulder strap or a cross-body strap, which should be longer. Measure around your body and tie a knot in the ends when you reach the desired length. Cut off any spare fabric as necessary.

Guess What...
Music Boxes

The first kind of portable music players were pocket-sized music boxes. Music boxes were tiny musical instruments carried in a box. You would turn a handle, which would crank a cylinder, which had a set of tiny pins set on it. The pins would pluck at a metal comb, which then created a musical tune. Music boxes were popular in the 1800s until the early twentieth century.

5 Place a dab of glue on either side of the T-shirt Music Player Holder. Press the ends of the strap onto each side of the holder and hold in place with clothespins while the glue dries.

You could also use fabric markers, glitter glue, or fabric stickers to decorate your Music Player Holder.

63

Patio Paint

Oh, the things you could create with Patio Paint! A game of hopscotch. A rainbow. Animals. A picture of a garden. A playground. The moon, stars, and a spaceship. Patio Paint can easily be made with just three ingredients which are found in most kitchen pantries. This is a Boredom Buster you'll want to do again and again every summer. Be sure to ask your parents for permission before you start painting.

MAKE IT IN: **15 minutes**
BOREDOM BUSTER: **One time activity (but you'll want to make it again)**
ACTIVITY LEVEL: ★

Things you need:

- 6-hole muffin pan (tin) or 6 clean, recycled yogurt containers
- Cornstarch (cornflour)
- Water
- Teaspoon
- Selection of food colorings
- Apron (or old T-shirt) for painting
- Sponges, foam brushes, or paintbrushes

1 Take your muffin pan (tin) and measure out two teaspoons of cornstarch (cornflour) into each hole. Alternatively, you can use clean yogurt containers.

2 Add two teaspoons of water to each hole and use a teaspoon to mix well so that there are no lumps.

3 Next, drop in 4–6 drops of food coloring into each hole. So, add four drops of red into one hole for red patio paint, four drops of blue into another for blue patio paint, four drops of green for the green patio paint, and so on. The more drops of food coloring you add, the bolder the color.

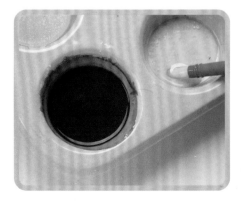

4 Put on an apron to protect your clothes while painting. Take your Patio Paint outside and start painting!

Tip

Fill a plastic container with water so you can clean your brushes between colors.

Guess What...
Cornstarch

Cornstarch is a fine white powder made from corn. Cornstarch is used for thickening foods and liquids. Baby powder often has cornstarch as one of its ingredients. It is called cornflour in the United Kingdom and called cornstarch in the United States of America and Canada. It is called *maizena* in French and *maicena* in Spanish.

Coffee and Tea Stained Tank Top

MAKE IT IN: **24 hours**

BOREDOM BUSTER: **One time activity (but you can make 4 shirts at a time)**

ACTIVITY LEVEL: ★ ★ ★

Things you need:

- Kettle
- Newspaper
- Large pan
- 12 tea bags
- 4 white cotton tank tops
- 12 tbsp instant coffee
- Spoon

To remove coffee stains from your pan, add one tablespoon of baking soda (bicarbonate of soda) and one tablespoon of water to the pan, and gently scrub the pan clean.

This is a cool activity to bust boredom on a summer day. Using the coffee and tea in your kitchen pantry, you can turn a regular white tank top into a custom designed one. Try creating stripes of color, or even an ombre design. This activity will also work with white cotton socks, white cotton tank tops, and white cotton kitchen towels.

1 Ask an adult to help you to boil a full kettle of water. Place sheets of newspaper under a large saucepan to protect your surface. Add 12 tea bags to the pan.

Stop for safety!
Ask an adult to help with boiling and pouring the hot water.

2 Pour the boiled water into the pan—you will need about 2 pints (1 liter). Let the tea steep for 30 minutes (it will turn dark brown).

3 Dunk the tops of the tank tops into the tea in the pan, allowing for the rest of the tank tops to hang outside the pot. Let soak for about 1 hour.

4 When the hour is up carefully take out the tank tops. Rinse with water over a sink until no color runs out. Wring out the tank top.

5 Bring another kettle of water to the boil. Meanwhile, throw away the tea in the pan and spoon the instant coffee into the pan.

6 Pour the boiled water into the pan and give it a stir. Take your tank tops and dunk them into the coffee in the pan, this time dipping the other end into the pan so that the tea-stained end is hanging outside the pan. Make sure you leave a strip of unstained tank top in the middle.

7 Leave the tank tops to sit in the coffee for about 1 hour and then repeat the instructions in step 4. Hang your tank tops up to dry, preferably outside in the sun.

Guess What... Cotton

Cotton grows on cotton plants. These plants grow in warm areas of countries like the United States of America, China, Pakistan, and India. Cotton fibers can be made into fabric. We use cotton fabric for clothes, sheets, towels, and more! Cottonseeds can be made into oils for cooking and cosmetics. Some animals eat cottonseeds as part of their diet.

CHAPTER 3
FALL

Permanent Marker Mugs

These permanent marker mugs are a fantastic, creative Boredom Buster. They also make great gifts, think: Mother's Day, Father's Day, teacher gift, Thank You gift, holiday gifts, and more! Need drawing ideas? You can draw a picture or cartoon, write a name or some song lyrics. Write a favorite quote or hashtag (#boredombusters). Write a word cloud (love, laugh, live). Or write a list with check mark boxes (hot chocolate, milk, tea).

MAKE IT IN: **3 hours**
BOREDOM BUSTER: **One time activity (but you can use it over and over again)**
ACTIVITY LEVEL: ★ ★ ★

Things you need:

- White ceramic mug
- Permanent marker pens (darker colors work best)
- Paper towel and water (for removing design if you want to change it)
- Cookie (baking) sheet
- Aluminum foil
- Oven timer (or clock with alarm)

1 DO NOT TURN THE OVEN ON YET. The finished cups need to go into a cold oven and then warm up as the oven warms up (to prevent the ceramic mugs from cracking). They also need to cool down as the oven cools down. Roll up your sleeves and remember that permanent marker stains clothing (but we know you'll be careful!).

2 Take your white ceramic mug and begin to draw your design with your permanent marker.

3 Be careful not to smudge the marker as you design. TIP: If there are smudges or if you are not happy with your design you can easily wipe your mug clean using a wet sheet of paper towel. You can only wipe away the permanent marker BEFORE the mug is baked.

4 Re-draw over your design a few times to make the lines bolder (the permanent marker will fade after it is baked).

5 Add colors and details to your design with permanent markers.

6 Place a sheet of aluminum foil on a cookie (baking) sheet and place your designed Permanent Marker Mugs on the foil.

7 Carefully place the cookie (baking) sheet onto a rack in a cold oven. Turn the oven on to 425°F (220°C/Gas 7). When the oven has reached this temperature, put the timer on for 30 minutes.

8 When the 30 minutes are up, turn off the oven. DO NOT OPEN THE DOOR. Allow the mugs to cool in the oven for two hours. Once cool, carefully remove the cookie sheet (baking tray) with the permanent marker mugs. To clean the mugs, wash carefully by hand.

Guess What...
Ceramics

Ceramics can be mugs, plates, figurines, bricks, tiles, and more. Ceramic comes from the Greek word *keramikos*, meaning pottery. An example of a ceramic is clay being shaped into a mug and then exposed to very high heat and then cooled down. Ceramics have been used for centuries as decorations and household items.

Recycled Cereal Box File Holder

This Recycled Cereal Box File Holder is a creative activity that helps keep your school stuff organized. Use it to keep track of your homework, school forms, library books, and more. It will also keep your favorite magazines and comic books organized.

 Use an empty cereal box to organize your things.

MAKE IT IN: **30 minutes**
BOREDOM BUSTER: **One time activity (but you can use it over and over)**
ACTIVITY LEVEL: ★ ★

Things you need:

• Large empty cardboard cereal box
• Scissors
• Ruler
• Marker pen
• Colorful duct tape

1 Lay your cereal box on a table. Using scissors, cut off the cardboard flaps at the top of the box so you have a nice neat edge.

2 Place the cereal box in front of you. Using a ruler and marker, mark a point about 4in (10cm) down from the top right corner. Now draw a straight line from the top left corner of the box down to the point you marked so you have a nice diagonal line.

3 Turn the box over and do the same on the other side, this time marking a point down from the top left corner and drawing a line from the top right corner to the marked point. Make sure you use the same measurement so your folder is the same on both sides. Join up the two diagonal lines by drawing a straight line along the side of the box.

4 Use scissors to cut along the first diagonal line, along the side, and then along the second diagonal line.

5 Now you are ready to decorate! Cut strips of duct tape and use them to cover the cardboard cereal box. TIP: Placing the duct tape strips vertically will mean less cutting and will be neater, as you can fold the ends inside the box. Done!

Guess What...
Cereal

Breakfast cereal was invented as a ready-to-eat breakfast to be served with cold milk. Before then people ate only hot cereals like oatmeal. Breakfast cereal can be made from corn, wheat, or rice. If you were a child in North America in the 1950s, you would have had a surprise because breakfast cereal makers put a toy in every breakfast cereal box! Toys included pencil toppers, bicycle wheel reflectors, football player cards, and more.

Greeting Card Bookmarks

Greeting Card Bookmarks are great to make in the fall because you can use them all through the school year. In this Boredom Buster, you recycle a favorite greeting card into something practical. Also, these Greeting Card Bookmarks can be fun holiday gifts to give to classmates—just write TO:... (their name) and FROM:... (your name) on the back of the bookmark.

Make old greeting cards into useful bookmarks.

MAKE IT IN: **20 minutes**
BOREDOM BUSTER: **One time activity (but you can use it over and over again)**
ACTIVITY LEVEL: ★

Things you need:

- Greeting card
- Scissors
- Hole punch
- Ribbon

1 Use a ruler and pencil to divide the front of the greeting card into long strips—you should be able to make about three bookmarks from one card. Each strip should be about 1¼in (3cm) wide.

2 Cut the greeting card into long strips.

3 Using a hole punch, punch a hole through the top of the card.

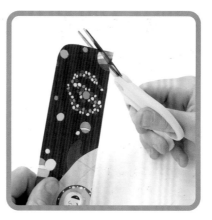

4 Cut a small length of ribbon and thread it through the hole to create a decorative knot.

5 If you prefer a bookmark with rounded edges, use a pair of scissors to round off the corners of the bookmark.

Guess What...
Bookmarks

In the 18th century the most common type of bookmark was a narrow silk ribbon attached to a book. In the Victorian age, young women embroidered bookmarks with needle and thread. Today, bookmarks can be made out of paper, leather, beads, paper clips, and more.

Spooky Cardboard Rolls

These Jack-O'-Lantern, Frankenstein's Monster, and Ghost cardboard rolls are easy and inexpensive Halloween paper crafts. Make one to decorate your desk or make a bunch and line them up to decorate your home or classroom.

Recycle cardboard toilet rolls to make fun, spooky characters.

MAKE IT IN: **20 minutes**
BOREDOM BUSTER: **One time activity (but it decorates all season)**
ACTIVITY LEVEL: ★

Things you need:

• Toilet roll tubes
• Orange, green, black, and white construction paper
• Scissors
• Sticky tape
• Black marker pen
• Hole punch (optional)
• Googly eyes

Jack-o'-lantern

1 Cut a piece of orange construction paper that is a bit longer and wider than your toilet roll tube. Line up the toilet roll tube along one edge of the paper and then stick the paper to the tube with a piece of sticky tape.

2 Roll the orange paper around the toilet roll tube and use another piece of tape to secure it in place.

3 Stand the tube upright and fold the top of the orange paper into the tube.

4 Now cut a strip of green construction paper that is about 1½in (4cm) wide and long enough to go around the toilet roll tube. Use scissors to make snips along one long edge of the paper (so that it looks like the top of a pumpkin).

5 Tape one end of the green paper to the top of the tube, wrap the paper around, and secure the end with another piece of sticky tape.

6 Use a black marker pen to draw a Jack-o'-lantern face: two triangle eyes, an upside-down triangle nose, and a scary mouth.

Guess What...
Pumpkins

Pumpkins are actually a fruit! They are related to squash, gourds, cucumbers, and melons. Pumpkins are grown in North America, Great Britain, and Europe. In general, pumpkins weigh 9–18lbs (4–8kg). Pumpkins can be made into soup, bread, or pie. Carved pumpkins are used as Halloween decorations and are called Jack-o'-lanterns.

Frankenstein's monster

1 Follow steps 1–3 of the Jack-o'-lantern, this time using green construction paper.

2 Cut a strip of black construction paper that is about 1½ in (4cm) wide and long enough to go around the toilet roll tube. Using scissors, cut out large and small triangles along one edge (this will be the monster's hair).

3 Use a hole punch to create two black paper circles for the eyes, and glue them onto the roll. Alternatively, use a black marker pen to draw two circles for the eyes. Finally, draw on a stitched or zigzag mouth.

Ghost

1 Follow steps 1–3 of the Jack-o'-lantern, this time using white construction paper.

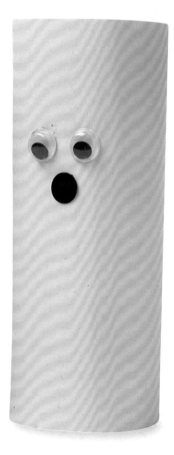

2 Glue on two googly eyes. Use a hole punch to create a black circle for the mouth, or draw it on with a marker pen.

Money Box

Piggy bank. Emergency fund. Mad money. Rainy day fund. Safe. Everyone needs a place to put their savings. This simple activity repurposes a clean cardboard canister into a coin container. It's a creative, practical Boredom Buster.

 Recycle an old cardboard container into a money box.

MAKE IT IN: 20 minutes
BOREDOM BUSTER: One time activity (but you can use it over and over again)
ACTIVITY LEVEL: ★

1 Wipe out the inside of your container with some kitchen paper and make sure the lid is clean and dry.

Things you need:

- Round cardboard tea or dry food container with a plastic lid (a square one will work fine too)
- Paper towel
- Colorful or patterned duct tape
- Scissors

2 Now take some colorful duct tape and wrap it around the outside of the container. Start at the top and make sure you line up the edge of the tape with the edge of the container for a nice neat finish.

3 Then, take the lid and carefully cut a slit—about the size of your biggest coin—into the top of the lid. (It might help to open the scissors out and push one point of the scissors through to get you started.) BE CAREFUL WHEN USING SCISSORS! Place the lid on top of your decorated Money Box and you're ready to start saving!

Guess What... Piggy Banks

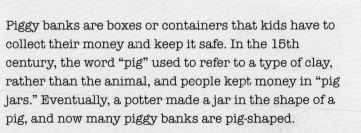

Piggy banks are boxes or containers that kids have to collect their money and keep it safe. In the 15th century, the word "pig" used to refer to a type of clay, rather than the animal, and people kept money in "pig jars." Eventually, a potter made a jar in the shape of a pig, and now many piggy banks are pig-shaped.

Halloween Silhouettes

Halloween Silhouettes are an easy and fun way to decorate your home or classroom for Halloween. Imagine footstep silhouettes walking up your wall... a witch silhouette taped to your window ... or a bat taped to your door! These are great do-it-yourself Halloween decorations!

MAKE IT IN: **30 minutes**
BOREDOM BUSTER: **One time activity**
ACTIVITY LEVEL: ★ ★

Things you need:

- Templates for witch, bat, and footsteps (see page 127)
- White computer paper
- Pencil
- Scissors
- Black construction paper
- Silver glitter paint or glitter glue (optional)
- Activity mat or newspaper (optional)

1 Photocopy the templates for the witch, bat, and footsteps onto white computer paper and then use scissors to carefully cut around the images.

2 Place each template onto a piece of black construction paper and use a pencil to trace around the images.

3 Now use scissors to cut out the witch, bat, and footsteps, from the black paper—you can cut as many Halloween Silhouettes as you like!

4 If you want to give your silhouettes some sparkle, decorate them with silver glitter paint or glitter glue, remembering to protect your surface with an activity mat or some newspaper.

Guess What...
Bats

There are about 900 types of bats worldwide. The bat is the only mammal that flies. Bats normally live in dark places like caves or hollow trees, and their fur is usually gray, black, or brown. Bats sleep while hanging upside down!

Banana Ghosts, Clementine Pumpkins, and Apple Smiles

Halloween foods are fun! What better way to get you in the holiday spirit than making some Banana Ghosts, Clementine Pumpkins, and Apple Smiles? These are great for after-school snacks, school lunches, and party food ideas. Trust me—you will be bewitched by these sweet treats!

MAKE IT IN: **20 minutes**

BOREDOM BUSTER: **One time activity (but you can make them over and over again)**

ACTIVITY LEVEL: ★ ★

Things you need:

- Apron
- Cutting board
- Knife
- Bananas
- Mini chocolate chips
- Regular-sized chocolate chips
- Clementines
- Celery
- Red-skinned apples
- Mini marshmallows
- Peanut butter (or nut-free spread)
- Plate

Stop for safety!
Ask an adult to help you when using a sharp knife.

1 Wash your hands, roll up your sleeves, and put on an apron to protect your clothes.

2 Start with the Banana Ghosts. Peel the banana and place it on your cutting board. Use a knife to cut the banana in half.

3 At the top (pointed) end of the banana half, push two mini chocolate chips for the ghost's eyes into the banana. Then insert one regular-sized chocolate chip under the eyes for the ghost's mouth.

4 To make the Clementine Pumpkins, peel the clementines but make sure you leave them whole. Try and get as much of the white pith off as possible.

Guess What...
Bananas

Bananas grow in tropical places like Africa, Asia, Central America, and South America. Bananas are grown on a banana plant (not a tree as some people think!). The banana plant can grow to 20ft (6m) tall. Each plant produces 50–150 bananas.

5 Cut a small piece of celery (about the size of the tip of your finger) and push it into the top of the peeled clementine.

6 For the Apple Smiles, cut a red-skinned apple into eight or ten sections (don't peel the apple—the red skins are the lips of your smiles). Take one piece of apple and spread some peanut butter (or nut-free spread) on one side.

7 Now stand five mini marshmallows side by side on the spread (these will be the teeth).

8 Finally, take another piece of apple, spread with some peanut butter, and lay this on top of the mini marshmallows.

9 Keep these Halloween treats in an airtight container in the fridge until you're ready to serve. Enjoy!

Backpack Tags

Backpack tags are a fantastic way to customize your backpack (and help find it quickly). You can design a backpack tag by drawing the first letter of your name or a creating a design which means something special to you, such as a motorcycle, football, or flower.

1 Lay your paper out on a flat surface. Using a ruler, measure and mark two rectangles each 4 x 3in (10 x 8cm) on the paper.

2 Using scissors, cut out the rectangles you just drew.

Cut up cereal boxes to use the cardboard.

MAKE IT IN: **20 minutes**
BOREDOM BUSTER: **One time activity (but keeps forever)**
ACTIVITY LEVEL: ★

Things you need:

- White or patterned craft paper
- Pencil and ruler
- Scissors
- Marker pens
- Stickers
- Cardboard (recycled cereal boxes are great for this!)
- Glue (or tape)
- Clear contact paper (sticky-backed plastic)
- Hole punch
- Ribbon or shoelace

3 If you are using plain white paper, use markers to decorate both rectangles—suggestions: a colored border, background lines, zigzags, shapes, your first name, the first letter of your name, or a favorite design. Alternatively, you can decorate the paper with some of your favorite stickers.

4 Next, cut a piece of cardboard that is the same size as your paper rectangles—4 x 3in (10 x 8cm).

5 Glue your designed paper rectangles to the front and back of the cardboard—this will make your backpack tag sturdier.

6 Now cut two pieces of clear contact paper (sticky-backed plastic) that are 4½ x 3½ in (11 x 9cm). Unpeel the backing from the contact paper and place it on a flat surface. Line up your backpack tag and place it in the center of the contact paper. Next, unpeel and place the top piece of contact paper over the top of the backpack tag.

7 Use scissors to trim off any extra contact paper around the edges of the tag.

8 Use a hole punch to make a hole in the top of your backpack tag.

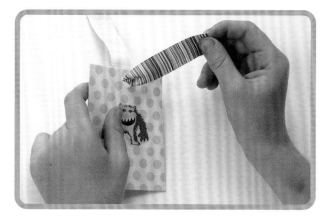

9 Measure a 5in (12cm) length of ribbon or shoelace, thread it through the hole, and tie it to your backpack zipper with a double knot.

Guess What...
Contact Paper

Contact paper (also known as sticky-backed plastic) is smooth on one side and extremely sticky on the other side. It is often used to line the bottoms of drawers and cabinets. Contact paper can come in bright colors with bold designs or can be clear—ideal for protecting book covers.

Switch up this Boredom Buster by making small and large backpack tags or by changing the shape from a rectangle to a circle.

Eyeball Wreath

An Eyeball Wreath is a frighteningly fun decoration for Halloween. Make one for your door, hang one in your room, or make a few to decorate your classroom. They are also great decorations for a Halloween-themed party.

MAKE IT IN: **30 minutes**
BOREDOM BUSTER: **One time activity (but lasts forever)**
ACTIVITY LEVEL: ★

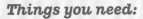

Things you need:

- Paper plate (a styrofoam plate works well too)
- 20 small styrofoam balls (available at craft stores)
- Black permanent marker
- Scissors
- White school glue (PVA glue)

1 First you need to cut out the center of your plate. The easiest way to do this is to start by cutting an "X" shape in the center of the plate.

2 You should be able to move your scissors more easily now. Cut around the inside of the plate, along the edge of the ridged part of the paper plate. You should be left with a wreath (or ring) shape. Keep the middle part of the plate to one side for now.

3 Next, take the small styrofoam balls and, using a black permanent marker, draw a small black circle on one side (this makes an eyeball).

4 Once all of the styrofoam balls have been made into eyes, squirt some glue around one half of the ridge of the paper plate wreath. Then, take a styrofoam ball and place it at the top, with the eyeball pointing out. Continue to place eyeballs on the glue (you'll need 10 for each half).

 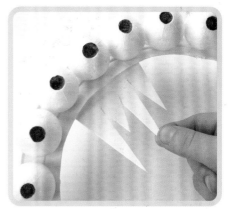

5 When you have glued half the plate with eyeballs, take your glue and squirt it around the other half of the paper plate wreath. Repeat to stick the remaining eyeballs on the glue.

6 Next, cut out two sets of teeth shapes from the middle part of the plate that you saved in step 2. Glue these to the back of your Eyeball Wreath. Lay the Eyeball Wreath on a flat surface and allow to dry for about 15 minutes.

Guess What...
Eyes

Humans have two eyeballs, which sit in openings in the skull. The skull protects the back and sides of the eyeballs. Eyelids protect the front of the eyeballs. Eyelashes protect eyeballs from dust and other tiny particles, which might go into the eyes. Blinking and tears keep eyes moist.

Ribbon Memo Board

This Ribbon Memo Board is a fun activity and an excellent organizational tool. Pin your school forms, invitations, favorite pictures, notes, and more. The activity works on both small and big corkboards, and is perfect for back-to-school sorting!

MAKE IT IN: **60 minutes**
BOREDOM BUSTER: **One time activity (but keeps forever)**
ACTIVITY LEVEL: ★ ★

Things you need:

- Cork bulletin board (available at office supply stores)
- Push pins (drawing pins)
- Wide ribbon
- Narrow ribbon
- Scissors
- Paper clips

Use paper clips to secure notes and other items to the wide ribbons at the top of the board. Slip photos and other mementoes into the criss-cross ribbons.

1 Find the center of your corkboard (a general guess will do). Using a push pin (drawing pin), pin the end of a piece of wide ribbon into the back of the corkboard. Stretch it around the front of the corkboard and then pin it to the other side (the back) of the board. Trim the end of the ribbon with scissors.

2 Turn the board over and push two more push pins into the ribbon, to secure it in place.

3 Repeat step 1 to pin more lengths of wide ribbon to the side of the first one. Depending on how big your board is, you might have three or four ribbons running across the board. Try and make them evenly spaced.

4 Now take your narrow ribbon and start making a criss-cross pattern on the other side of the wide ribbon in the center of the board. Do this by pinning ribbon at an angle, starting at the left-hand side of the center ribbon line and going down to the bottom right edge of the board. Then pin another piece of ribbon going the other way.

5 Keep adding pieces of ribbon in a criss-cross pattern, pinning at the top and bottom to hold in place. Insert push pins at each intersection (where two ribbons meet) to secure them in place.

6 Trim the ends of the ribbons with scissors.

Guess What... Cork

Cork is made from the bark of the cork oak tree grown in Portugal, Spain, and North Africa. The tree can grow up to 60ft (18m) tall. The cork oak bark is cut off, dried, and boiled. Cork can be used to seal bottles, keep houses warm, used for shoe soles—and turned into bulletin boards!

Shoe-box Jewelry Box

This terrific activity busts boredom, recycles something meant for the trash bin, and helps you organize your jewelry in an inexpensive way! This Shoe-box Jewelry Box is meant to stand up on its end so your necklaces can hang down.

Reuse an old shoebox to make a pretty storage box.

MAKE IT IN: **30 minutes**
BOREDOM BUSTER: **One time activity (but keeps forever)**
ACTIVITY LEVEL: ★ ★

Things you need:

* Cardboard shoe box
* Colorful gift wrap
* Scissors
* Glue or sticky tape
* Ruler and pencil
* Ribbon
* Glitter glue, marker pens, buttons, ribbon, or fabric pieces (optional)

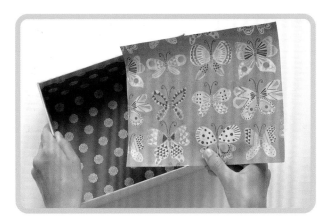

1 Take your cardboard shoe box and cover the outside in colorful gift wrap. If the inside of your box is a solid color you won't need to cover it but if there are any words or designs you should cover them with paper. Use glue or sticky tape to stick the paper down.

2 Using a ruler and pencil, measure and mark 1 in (2.5cm) in and 1 in (2.5cm) down from the top left corner of the box. Repeat at the top right of the box.

3 Use scissors to poke a hole on the right and left sides of the box where you marked. Be sure to poke through the card and the gift wrap on the back.

4 Cut a piece of ribbon 12in (30cm) long and thread it through the hole on the left from the inside of the box. Tie a double knot on the outside of the box so the knot doesn't slip through the hole. Take the other end of the ribbon and thread it through the right hole and tie a double knot on the outside of the box. Trim off any extra ribbon. You can now tie your necklaces around the ribbon to keep them from getting tangled.

5 If you have used a large box you may have space to add another ribbon near the bottom of the box to keep your bracelets organized. If you want to decorate the outside of your box, use glitter glue, marker pens, buttons, ribbons, or fabric pieces—it's up to you!

Experiment with different sizes—you can use something as small as a tissue box or go for something much bigger!

Guess What...
Shoe Boxes

In the 1600s in North America, shoes were made and repaired by cobblers. Cobblers went from town to town making shoes on demand for paying customers. Later, shoemakers set up shops in villages and people would go to them to have shoes made and repaired. These days, shoes are made in vast quantities at factories, where cardboard shoe boxes are used to store, protect, and ship shoes from the factory to a store.

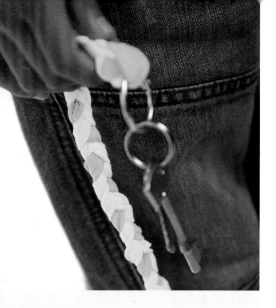

T-shirt Key Chain

Recycle your worn T-shirts to make this braided key chain. It's fun, easy, and really inexpensive! It's a great project to do by yourself or as an activity to do with your friends. These would make a fun gift for your teacher or for Mother's Day, Father's Day, or any other day!

Recycle old clothes into fun accessories.

MAKE IT IN: 30 minutes
BOREDOM BUSTER: One time activity (but you can use it again and again)
ACTIVITY LEVEL: ★

Things you need:

- Activity mat
- 2 clean, worn T-shirts in different colors
- Metal key ring loop
- Superglue
- Scissors

It's fine if your T-shirts have stains as the braiding will hide them. Adult size T-shirts will make long key chains, children's size T-shirts will make medium-sized key chains, and toddler size T-shirts will make shorter key chains.

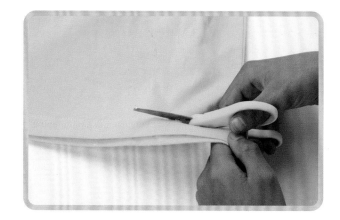

1 Roll up your sleeves and place your activity mat on a flat surface. Cut three strips of T-shirt fabric approximately 1 in (2.5cm) wide along the base of the T-shirt.

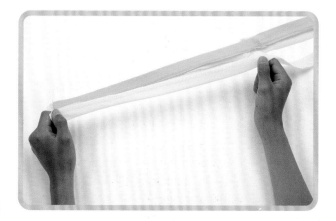

2 Line up the T-shirt strips (you need two of one color and one of another color) and pull them gently to lengthen them.

3 Next, tie a knot about 1½ in (4cm) from the top, tying the three pieces of T-shirt fabric together. Start braiding the pieces of T-shirt fabric. To do this, move the strip at the right over the strip in the middle, then move the strip at the left over the strip in the middle. Keep going until you reach the end. Tie a knot about 1½ in (4cm) from the bottom of the T-shirt fabric.

4 Thread the 1½ in (4cm) of unbraided T-shirt fabric through the metal key ring loop. Carefully apply superglue to both the braided and unbraided fabric, sticking it together. Apply a little more superglue to the sides and top to secure it in place. Leave the glue to dry for about 20 minutes. Use scissors to trim off any extra fabric at the bottom knotted end of the T-shirt fabric.

Guess What...
Largest T-shirt

In 2011 clothing manufacturer Gildan displayed the largest T-shirt ever in Nashville, USA. It measured 281⅓ ft (85.74m) in length and was 180⅞ ft (55.14m) wide. That's almost as big as a soccer (football) field! The T-shirt was then recycled to make 12,000 shirts, which were donated to school music programs in Nashville.

Stop for safety!
Ask an adult to help you when using superglue.

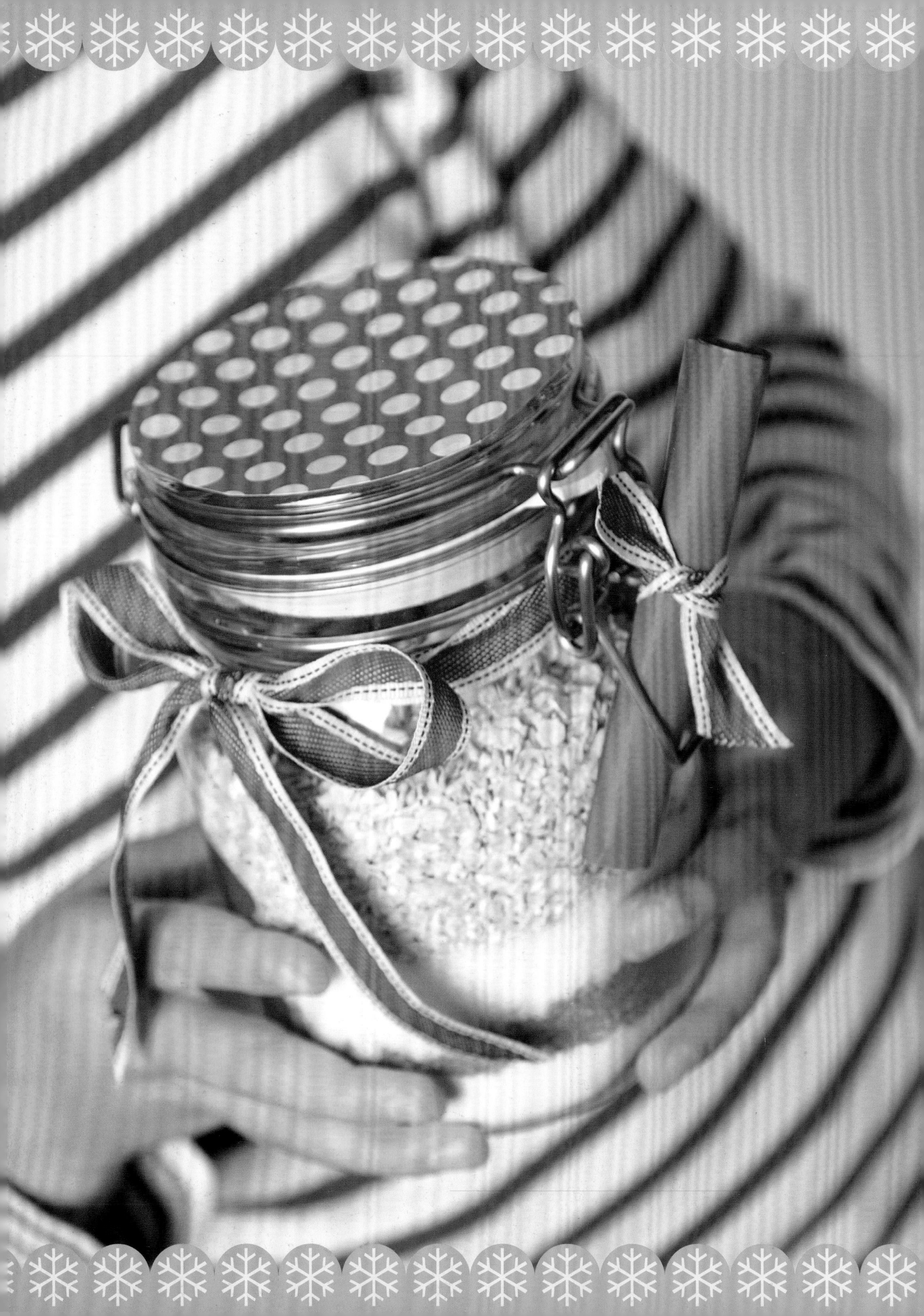

CHAPTER 4
WINTER

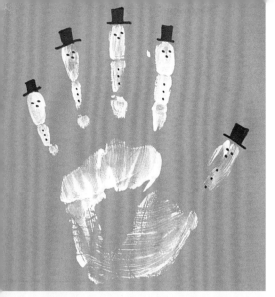

Snowman Handprints

Handprint art is especially fun in the winter, on those cold days when you are stuck inside and in need of a Boredom Buster! These Snowman Handprints are a fantastic winter art activity and holiday decoration. You could even scan the finished pictures into your computer, print them onto cards, and turn them into a holiday greeting card!

Recycle a clean yogurt container as a paint pot.

MAKE IT IN: **30 minutes**
BOREDOM BUSTER: **One time activity (but you can use it as a decoration over and over)**
ACTIVITY LEVEL: ★

Things you need:

• Apron
• Activity mat
• Colored construction paper
• White washable paint
• Paint pot
• Paintbrush
• Black permanent marker

1 Put on an apron, roll up your sleeves, and tie up your hair. Place a piece of colored construction paper on top of your activity mat and pour some white washable paint into a paint pot.

2 Using your paintbrush, paint the underside of your palm, fingers, and thumb with the white paint.

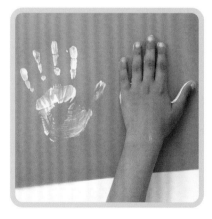

3 Next, press your painted hand gently yet firmly onto the colored construction paper. Carefully peel your hand away, then repeat to make another print, adding more paint to your hand if you think you need it. Leave the prints to dry for about 10 minutes.

4 When the paint is dry, take a black permanent marker. At the fingerprint tips draw a black top hat (a square shape with a long line underneath).

5 Next, draw a snowman face by drawing dots for the eyes, nose, and mouth. Finally, draw the snowman buttons (three dots in a line). Done!

Guess What...
Top Hats

Black top hats became a fashion trend for gentlemen in the late 1700s. Top hats could be made of beaver fur, silk, or felt. Famous wearers of top hats include Abraham Lincoln (the 16th President of the United States of America), the Mad Hatter (from *Alice in Wonderland*), and Willy Wonka (from *Charlie and the Chocolate Factory*).

No-sew Cinnamon Mats

This super-scented, no-sew craft is oh so easy! When a warm mug or cup is placed on the finished No-sew Cinnamon Mat the spice mixture inside smells delicious. It is such an easy (and inexpensive!) activity. Why not make four mats, using the same patterned fabric for each, so that you have a whole set of them?

MAKE IT IN: **60 minutes**
BOREDOM BUSTER: **One time activity (but you can use it over and over)**
ACTIVITY LEVEL: ★★

Things you need:

- Cotton fabric scraps— 5 x 5-in (13 x 13-cm) squares are ideal
- Scissors
- ½ cup (50g) ground cinnamon
- ½ cup (50g) ground allspice
- Felt (available from craft stores)
- White school glue (PVA glue)
- Teaspoon
- Small bowl

1 If you are using one large piece of fabric, cut it into 5 x 5-in (13 x 13-cm) squares (you will need two squares for each mat).

2 Combine the cinnamon and allspice together in a small bowl and mix together.

3 Place two squares of fabric in front of you, right (pattern) side down.

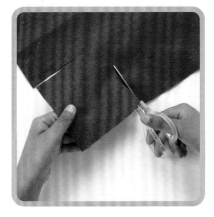

4 Next, cut a square of felt slightly smaller than your fabric square (you want to create a border area about the size of your fingertip).

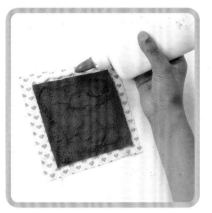

5 Place the square of felt on top of one square of fabric, then place a spoonful of the cinnamon and allspice mixture onto the center of the felt.

6 Carefully spread the spice mixture over the felt using a teaspoon—you don't need it to go right to the edges. Now take your glue and glue around the fabric square (in the border area between the felt and the outside edge of the fabric).

Guess What...
Allspice ?

Allspice comes from the dried berries of an evergreen tree that is found in the West Indies and Central America. It is named allspice because it smells like a combination of cloves, cinnamon, and nutmeg, so it smells like "all" spices. Allspice trees can grow to the height of 30ft (9m). Allspice is often used in cakes, cookies, stews, and seasonings.

7 Next, take the second piece of fabric and place it on top of the spice/felt square, with the right (pattern) side facing up. Glue may bubble out at the sides but simply spread it along the edge of the fabric with your finger. It will dry clear. Leave your No-sew Cinnamon Mat to dry for about 30 minutes.

If you want your No-sew Cinnamon Mat to be a bit more padded, use two squares of felt instead of one so you have a sandwich of fabric, felt, spices, felt, fabric!

3D Valentines

3D Valentines are a fun twist on heart-shaped paper crafts. String a few of them together to make a Valentine's Day garland, thread one with string for a hanging decoration, or write your name on one and give it as a homemade Valentine for a friend or classmate.

MAKE IT IN: **15 minutes**
BOREDOM BUSTER: **One time activity (but you can do it over and over again)**
ACTIVITY LEVEL: ★ ★

Things you need:

• 4 sheets of colored computer or construction paper
• Pencil
• Scissors
• Stapler
• White school glue (PVA glue)
• String or ribbon (optional)

Stop for safety!
Ask an adult to help you when using the scissors.

1 Start by making a heart-shaped stencil. Take a sheet of paper and fold it in half.

2 Take a pencil and draw half of a heart shape on one side of the folded paper. Start your heart shape in the middle of the folded edge, draw a line upward, around, and then back down to the folded edge.

3 Take your scissors and cut along the heart-shaped pencil line. When you open out the fold, you will have a perfectly even heart shape.

4 You can either use this heart shape as your stencil by drawing around it on the remaining three sheets of paper, OR you can put three sheets of paper together, fold them, and repeat step 2. Cut out all the hearts.

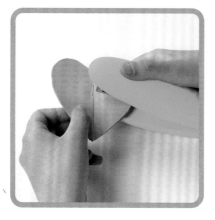  

5 Next, you need to connect the four hearts. Arrange the four hearts one on top of the other and staple them in the middle— two staples should be enough.

6 Then, gently separate the paper hearts, folding and pulling each layer of paper until you have a 3D shape.

7 OPTIONAL: If you want to hang your heart, take a piece of narrow ribbon or string, fold it in half to make a loop, and glue the two ends to the middle part of the heart.

Guess What...
Hearts

The human heart is not heart-shaped at all. It's actually more of a pear shape and is about the size of your fist. The heart is made of strong muscle and pumps blood through your body from head to toe. On average, the heart muscle beats 70 times per minute. Keep your heart strong by eating a healthy diet and exercising regularly.

Juice Box Snowmen

Making Juice Box Snowmen is a fun Boredom Buster for a winter afternoon. You can make one for your desk or make a few and line them up in a row to decorate your table, window, or mantelpiece. Juice Box Snowmen are really easy and inexpensive to make and encourage recycling.

 Clean and reuse cardboard juice boxes.

MAKE IT IN: **20 minutes**
BOREDOM BUSTER: **One time activity (but it decorates all season long)**
ACTIVITY LEVEL: ★

Things you need:

- Empty mini cardboard juice box container
- White, black, and orange construction paper
- Scissors
- Sticky tape
- Hole punch
- White school glue (PVA glue)

1 Ensure your cardboard juice box container is completely empty. It's a good idea to leave it upside down in the kitchen sink overnight.

2 Take a piece of white construction paper, fold it in half, and cut along the fold to make two halves. Take one half and place the cardboard juice box on top of it, lining it so that the bottom of the juice box lines up with the bottom of the construction paper.

Guess What... Juice Boxes

In 1963 a Swedish man named Ruben Rausing invented a new way to package and store milk in cardboard, rather than glass or plastic. His rectangular, milk package was called the "Tetra Brik." You can now find large and small Tetra Briks all over the world.

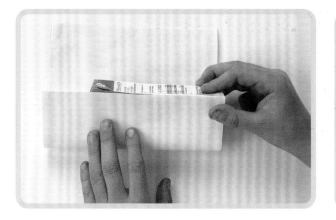 

3 Tape the white construction paper to the cardboard juice box at one edge and then roll the construction paper around the juice box. Use sticky tape to secure the construction paper in place.

4 Next, cut two small pieces of tape and tape the bottom sides of the construction paper to the juice box (this will make sure it doesn't fall out when you move it).

 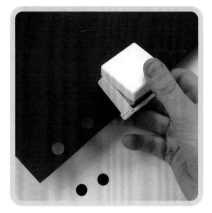 

5 Fold in the two sides of construction paper at the top of the juice box, then fold in the front and back. Tape the paper down.

6 Next, use a hole punch to punch out circles from the black construction paper—you need two circles for the "coal" eyes and four circles for the mouth.

7 Using scissors, cut out a small triangle from the orange construction paper (for a carrot nose).

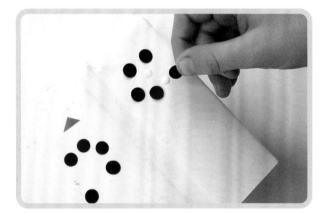

8 Put dots of glue where you would like to place the eyes, nose, and mouth and then carefully place your circles and triangle on the glue to make a snowman face.

9 Finally, use scissors to cut out a top hat from the black construction paper and stick it onto your snowman.

To cut out a top hat, simply draw a rectangle (for the bottom of the hat), and a square above it (for the top).

Salt Dough

Salt Dough is a fun and frugal activity, which uses ingredients you probably already have in your kitchen or classroom! Baked salt dough can keep for years in an airtight container. This Boredom Buster shows how you can use salt dough in the winter but you can also use it in other seasons, think: spring flowers, summer butterflies, or fall leaves.

MAKE IT IN: **2½ hours**
BOREDOM BUSTER: **One time activity (but you can use it over and over again)**
ACTIVITY LEVEL: ★★★

Things you need:

- ½ cup (120g) fine salt
- ½ cup (50g) flour (any kind)
- ¼ cup + 2 tbsp (100ml) water
- Measuring cups
- Bowl
- Mixing spoon
- Cookie (baking) sheet
- Parchment paper
- Straw (optional)
- Paints and paintbrush or permanent marker pens

1 Preheat the oven to 200°C (400°F/Gas 6). Measure out the salt, flour, and water and pour into a bowl.

2 Using a spoon, mix the ingredients together—it will start off very crumbly.

3 When it starts to look like dough, get your hands in the bowl and knead it.

4 Line a cookie (baking) sheet with parchment paper.

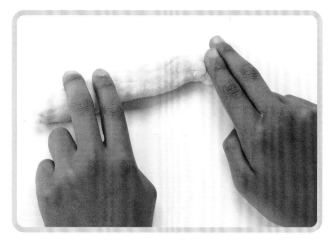

5 Using your hands, roll bits of salt dough into balls.

6 To make snowmen: roll out three ball shapes (small, medium, and large) and stack them on top of each other. To make trees: roll out a ball shape and press it down and then cut a triangle shape. To make candy canes: take some salt dough in your hands and roll it like a snake, then place it on the parchment paper and curl the top to make the "hook."

7 You can roll, shape, and play with the dough over and over until you have a decoration you like—it will only set hard once it is baked. Place your Salt Dough shapes on the lined cookie (baking) sheet.

Guess What...
Minerals

Minerals are elements which do not come from animals or plants, making them inorganic substances. Minerals are found deep inside the Earth as well as on the Earth's surface. Rocks, soil, and sand are all made from minerals. They come in many different colors and well-known minerals include salt, gold, diamond, and silver.

8 If you want hanging Salt Dough decorations, use a straw and poke a hole in the top of your decoration before you bake it. Ask an adult to help you to put the cookie (baking) sheet in the preheated oven. Bake the salt dough for 2 hours.

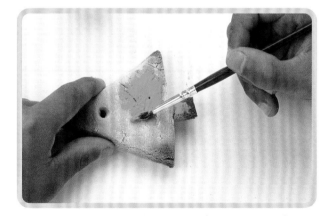

9 Once cooked and cooled, use colored paints or permanent marker pens to decorate your Salt Dough figures.

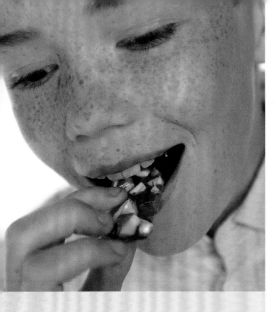

Candy Cane Chocolate Bark

Delicious, simple, and inexpensive, this is a great dessert to make for any winter party. It is called Candy Cane Chocolate Bark because it looks a bit like tree bark (only more yummy). You can experiment with your own versions of this by replacing the candy canes with mini marshmallows, chocolate-covered candies, white chocolate chunks, nuts, or dried fruit.

MAKE IT IN: **60 minutes**
BOREDOM BUSTER: **One time activity (but you can make it over and over again)**
ACTIVITY LEVEL: ★ ★ ★

Things you need:

• Apron
• Parchment paper
• Cookie (baking) sheet
• 2 large (or 4 small) candy canes
• Resealable plastic bag
• Large wooden spoon
• 1 cup (180g) chocolate chips
• Microwave-safe bowl
• Spatula

1 Roll up your sleeves, put an apron on, and wash your hands. Place a sheet of parchment paper on a cookie (baking) sheet.

Stop for safety!
Ask an adult to help you use the microwave.

2 Put the candy canes into the plastic bag and seal it. Using the back of a wooden spoon, carefully smash the candy canes into teeny tiny pieces.

Guess What... Bark

The outer layer of a tree trunk is called bark. Bark is very important to trees. It keeps the water inside the tree from escaping. Bark protects the tree from possible injuries, which could be made by the weather, animals, or even people.

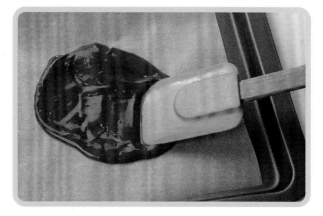

3 Measure out the chocolate chips and put them in microwave-safe bowl. Ask an adult to help you microwave the chocolate chips on high until melted—this will take about 60 seconds but microwave them in 20-second bursts as chocolate can burn easily. Be careful when checking, as the chocolate will be very hot.

4 When the chocolate chips are all melted, carefully remove the microwave-safe bowl from the microwave and then pour the melted chocolate onto the parchment paper, using a spatula to scrape out all the chocolate.

5 Use the spatula to spread the melted chocolate into a rectangle shape. Then, open the plastic bag and sprinkle the candy cane pieces all over the top of the rectangle.

6 Place the cookie (baking) sheet in the freezer for 30 minutes. When the chocolate has hardened, break the Candy Cane Chocolate Bark into pieces (some big and some small). Candy Cane Chocolate Bark will keep in an airtight container for a few weeks in the fridge—if you can keep it that long!

Tissue Box Desk Organizer

This Tissue Box Desk Organizer encourages recycling. Turn a cardboard box and some cardboard toilet roll tubes into a fun and functional desk organizer for your pens, pencils, and school supplies. You could even invite people to tuck notes inside of the toilet paper rolls and use it as a mailbox!

 Recycle an empty tissue box and toilet roll tubes, too.

MAKE IT IN: **20 minutes**

BOREDOM BUSTER: **One time activity (but you can use it over and over again)**

ACTIVITY LEVEL: ★★

Things you need:

- Empty tissue box
- Duct tape (look for colored or patterned tape and use an assortment)
- 3 toilet roll tubes
- Scissors

There is no need for any measuring with this Boredom Buster—simply pull and stick the duct tape from the roll and cut it off at the end.

1 Tape strips of duct tape around the top of the tissue box, making sure you keep the open hole at the top clear of tape. Trim the ends with scissors.

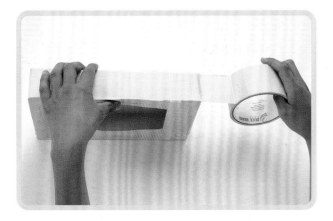

2 Next, attach the end of the duct tape to the top side of the box and pull the duct tape all the way around the box, gently pressing on it to stick it down. Cover all four sides in this way. You don't need to cover the bottom as it won't be seen but you can if you want to!

3 Next, take a toilet roll tube and stick a strip of duct tape around the top of the tube.

4 Add another strip of duct tape all around the toilet roll tube, this time sticking it just under the first strip of tape. Add more duct tape so that you are creating a striped effect. Repeat to cover the other two toilet roll tubes.

5 Then, insert the toilet roll tubes one-by-one into the top opening of the tissue box. They will stand up on their own. Fill the toilet roll tubes with your pens, scissors, and school supplies.

Guess What...
Handkerchiefs

Before tissues were invented people used handkerchiefs to wipe their faces or blow their noses. Instead of using tissue boxes people carried handkerchiefs in their pockets. Handkerchiefs are squares of fabric often made out of cotton or silk. In 1785, French King Louis XVI (married to Marie Antoinette, Archduchess of Austria and Queen of France) made a law that said handkerchiefs must be square shaped (and they have remained so ever since).

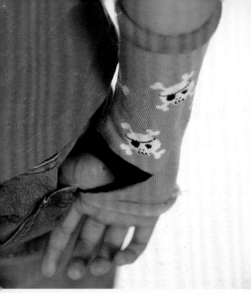

Sock Arm Warmer

Making a Sock Arm Warmer is a fun activity for a chilly afternoon. It mixes creativity with purpose, making something which will keep you warm. You can use matched or odd socks: try it—it's fun! The secret? You must use knee-length socks to make Sock Arm Warmers.

 Recycle clean socks into these arm warmers.

MAKE IT IN: **15 minutes**
BOREDOM BUSTER: **One time activity (but you can use them over and over again)**
ACTIVITY LEVEL: ★

Things you need:

- Clean knee socks
- Scissors
- Ruler
- Pencil or washable marker

1 Lay your knee socks out on a flat surface.

2 Use a ruler and pencil to mark a straight line across the sock, about 1in (2.5cm) below the heel section of the sock.

3 Use the scissors to cut across this line. The sock fabric might roll down a bit but this is perfectly fine.

4 Next, use your ruler to measure and mark a triangle 1in (2.5cm) in at the heel section of the sock. The base of the triangle will be at the outside heel and the point of the triangle will be pointing inside the sock. Cut out the triangle using scissors. Repeat with the other sock.

Guess What...
Socks

Socks come from the Latin word *soccus*, meaning a slipper. Historians have found knitted socks in Egyptian tombs, dating back to the third century. These days we wear many different kinds of socks: sports socks, knee socks, casual socks, non-slip socks, and even toe socks.

5 Finally, pull the socks over your hands and up your arms. The triangle you created in the sock heel becomes a thumbhole and the end of the sock lies just at your knuckles.

Try looking for suitable socks in thrift stores, or perhaps you have a few at the bottom of the laundry basket that are missing their partner? You could also use socks that have worn through at the toe.

Sock Mug Warmer

Ever picked up a cup filled with a hot drink and found the cup too hot to hold? This Boredom Buster reuses those lonely socks in the bottom of the laundry basket into a practical item that keeps your drinks warm and your fingers cool.

MAKE IT IN: **20 minutes**
BOREDOM BUSTER: **One time activity (but keeps forever)**
ACTIVITY LEVEL: ★ ★

Things you need:

• Clean sock (a wool sock works best)
• Scissors
• Cup without a handle (for measuring your Sock Mug Warmer)

1 Lay out your wool sock on a flat surface. Lay the cup next to the opening at the top of the sock. If there is a design at the top of the sock, such as a stripe, position the cup below the design so that you can fold it over when it is on the mug and show off the design.

2 Use a pair of scissors to cut off the bottom of the sock, just below where the bottom of the cup will be. Put the bottom part of your sock in your craft bin for future Boredom Busters.

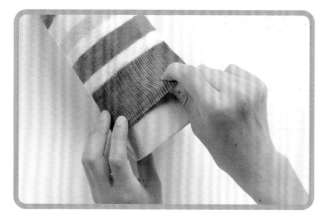

3 Slip your Sock Mug Warmer over your cup, pulling it almost up to the top of the cup.

4 Sew on buttons around the top of the mug warmer for extra decoration.

Guess What...
Wool

Wool is a fiber that covers animals like sheep, goats, and camels. Wool protects these animals from heat and cold. Wool is produced in the United Kingdom, Australia, China, and New Zealand. Wool is sheared (sheared means trimmed) off the animals and is then used to make clothing, carpets, craft supplies, and more.

The Sock Mug Warmer is also great to keep in your bag for those times when you get a hot drink on-the-go.

Easy No-sew Hat

This Easy No-sew Hat is a cool Boredom Buster and a definite must-try! If you can tie a knot you can make this fleece hat. The secret? Be sure to tie a double knot each time so that the knot stays put! You can find polar fleece at fabric stores.

MAKE IT IN: **30 minutes**
BOREDOM BUSTER: **One time activity (but can be worn again and again)**
ACTIVITY LEVEL: ★★

Things you need:

- Polar fleece—18in (46cm) will make two child-size hats
- Scissors
- Tape measure
- An old hat (one which already fits you)

Stop for safety!
Ask an adult to help you when using scissors.

1 Polar fleece stretches more one way than the other. Start by stretching your polar fleece to see which way it stretches the most. Whichever way it stretches more, place your fabric so the stretch is from side to side. This will make the knotting much easier.

2 Fold the polar fleece over so that the fold is at the top and you now have a double layer of fleece in front of you.

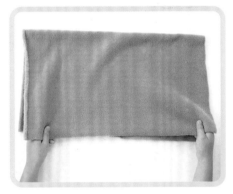

3 Lay an old hat on top of your polar fleece. Measure 2in (5cm) either side of the widest part of your old hat (usually the bottom or brim of the hat). Measure and cut a square from the fleece 2in (5cm) bigger around your old hat.

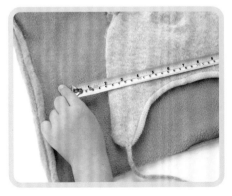

4 Next, every 2in (5cm) along the right side of the hat, cut a 2in (5cm) line through both the top and bottom layers of polar fleece. Repeat these cuts on the left side of the hat. The fabric will remain a square shape (but with a 2in/5cm fringe).

5 Now you are ready to start knotting! Take the top layer of polar fleece and double knot it with the bottom layer of polar fleece, matching up the 2in (5cm) cuts. Knot up the fringe on both sides of the hat. Double knotting is very important!

Guess What...
Coldest Day Ever Recorded

The coldest day ever recorded on Earth was August 2010, in East Antarctica, when the temperature was recorded, by satellite, at minus 136°F (minus 93.2°C). That was a day you needed a warm hat! The chilly discovery was made by NASA (National Aeronautics and Space Administration) scientists.

Gift in a Jar

A Gift in a Jar is an easy, inexpensive idea, which is great for any occasion. This stress-free Boredom Buster combines the activities of measuring, pouring, writing, and decorating. This project makes a gift of the ingredients and recipe for oatmeal chocolate candy cookies, but you can switch up this activity by using things like dry soup ingredients, brownie ingredients, or cake ingredients.

MAKE IT IN: **30 minutes**
BOREDOM BUSTER: **One
   time activity**
ACTIVITY LEVEL: ★

Things you need:

- Large glass jar with lid
- Measuring cups
- Teaspoon
- 1⅓ cups (130g) all-purpose (plain) flour
- 1 tsp baking powder
- 1 tsp baking soda (bicarbonate of soda)
- ¼ tsp salt
- ½ cup (100g) brown sugar
- ½ cup (100g) white sugar
- 1⅓ cups (100g) rolled oats
- ½ cup (85g) candy-coated chocolates such as M&M's or Smarties
- Recipe card or colorful paper
- Pencil, pen, or marker
- Sticky tape
- Scissors
- Ribbon
- Colored paper for lid decoration (optional)

1 Wash your jar and lid and then dry them really well. Wash your hands.

2 Using your measuring cups and teaspoon, measure out the ingredients one by one and layer them on top of each other, in the order listed, in the large glass jar. Use the back of a spoon to pack the sugar down. Put the lid on the jar and close tightly.

Guess What... Glass

It is believed that the Ancient Egyptians made glass jars as long ago as 2,500 BC! European churches started using stained glass in windows in the 1100s. In 1608, people in the American colonies started to make glass. We now have glass containers for food and drink, glass mirrors, and glass lenses among many everyday glass objects—what would we do without it!

 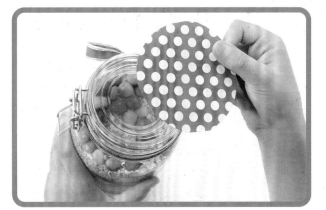

3 Take a recipe card or a piece of colorful paper that is roughly 6 x 4in (15 x 10cm). Write the following instructions on the card, in pencil, pen, or marker pen: "Preheat the oven to 350°F (180°C/Gas 4). Line a cookie sheet with non-stick parchment paper. Pour the contents of this jar into a large bowl and add ½ cup of melted butter, 1 egg, and 1 teaspoon of vanilla extract. Mix well. Spoon dollops of mixture onto the cookie sheet and bake in the oven for 10–12 minutes. Enjoy!"

4 Roll up the recipe card so it looks like a scroll, tie it with a ribbon, and attach it (using sticky tape) to the large glass jar. Then tie a large ribbon around the top of the glass jar. If you want you can also cut a circle of colored paper to cover the lid of the jar for an extra decoration.

Jar Lid Magnets

In this Boredom Buster you can découpage (see page 27) jar lids and turn them into these Jar Lid Magnets to decorate your fridge for the holidays. This is a great indoor activity for a chilly winter day.

Collect used metal jar lids and repurpose them into something cool!

MAKE IT IN: 1¼ hours (includes drying time)
BOREDOM BUSTER: One time activity (but you can do several at a time)
ACTIVITY LEVEL: ★★

Things you need:

- Activity mat or newspaper
- Old magazines, pictures printed from a computer, gift wrap, or greeting cards
- Scissors
- Metal jar lids
- White school glue (PVA glue)
- Container for glue (a clean yogurt container is ideal)
- Paintbrush
- Magnets (available from craft stores)

1 Go through your old magazines, gift wrap, or greeting cards and look for any winter-themed pictures— think: snowflakes, trees, reindeer, snowmen, toboggan, mittens, winter hats, scarves. They will need to fit on top of the jar lids so don't choose anything too big. Trace around the jar lid over your chosen pictures and carefully cut them out with the scissors.

2 Protect your work surface with an activity mat or some newspaper. Pour one teaspoon of glue into a container. Add a teaspoon of water and stir well to mix. This will make a small amount of découpage glue— if you want to make a lot of Jar Lid Magnets, you will need more glue. Just use equal quantities of glue and water and mix well.

3 Using a paintbrush, brush a layer of the glue/water mixture on top of the metal jar lids. You can découpage either side of the lids—it's up to you.

4 Next, place your winter picture cutouts on top of the glued side of the metal jar lids. Brush another layer of the glue/water mixture on top of the cutouts (don't worry—it will dry clear). Be sure to brush the edges and use your fingers to press down if needed to ensure the edges are attached to the metal jar lid.

5 Allow the jar lids to dry—this may take up to an hour. When the lids are dry, glue a magnet to the other side of the lid.

Guess What... Metals ?

The first metals to be discovered were gold and copper. The next metals discovered were silver, lead, tin, and iron. Some metals are found within the Earth's crust and others are man-made. Metals can be hammered into shape or heated until they become liquid and poured into molds to take a shape. Metals can be used in jewelry, building construction, car manufacturing, furniture, household appliances, and much more.

Paper Snowflakes

This simple paper craft makes a great winter decoration for the home or classroom. Snowflakes make beautiful window decorations, card decorations, and hanging ornaments. Like real snowflakes, these paper snowflakes are unique as you cut each one a little differently, making each one of a kind.

MAKE IT IN: **15 minutes**
BOREDOM BUSTER: **One time activity**
ACTIVITY LEVEL: ★ ★ ★

Things you need:

• White paper (computer paper will work fine)
• Scissors

Fun fact: even though no two snowflakes are ever the same, snowflakes always have six sides or points. This is to do with the way the crystals form.

1 Place a sheet of paper in front of you, so that the long edges of the rectangle are top and bottom. You need to turn this rectangle into a square so take the bottom right corner of the paper and fold it up so that the right edge of the paper lines up with the top edge of the paper, making a triangle. Press along the diagonal fold with your fingers.

2 Next, use scissors to cut off the paper on the right that is not part of the triangle—it is a long rectangle of paper. (Why not decorate this leftover strip of paper and use it as a bookmark?)

3 Now lay the triangle in front of you with the long edge at the bottom and fold in half so you have a smaller triangle.

Stop for safety!
Ask an adult to help you when using scissors.

4 Then you need to fold the triangle into thirds. With the long edge at the bottom, take the right-hand corner of your triangle and fold it over to the center so you have a straight line going down from the tip of the triangle. Press the fold with your fingers.

Guess What...
Snowflakes

Snowflakes are actually a collection of ice crystals clumped together. One snowflake can be made from up to 100 ice crystals. Snowflakes are created in clouds—when it is cold, the water vapor in a cloud freezes into ice crystals, forming snow. When the snowflakes are heavy enough they fall to the ground.

5 Now take the left-hand side of the triangle and fold it all the way over so that you have a thinner triangle with an uneven bottom (a bit like a rocket ship!). You may need to adjust the creases and folds so that you have a nice neat triangle with all the edges lined up.

6 Using scissors, cut a diagonal line at the bottom of the triangle. This will create the all-important six points of the snowflake.

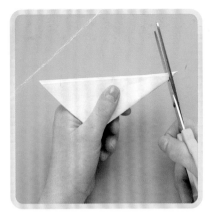

7 Use scissors to cut off the very tip of the triangle—this will be the center of your snowflake.

8 Now you are ready to starting cutting out your designs! Cut hearts, squares, triangles, semicircles, and diamonds along the folded edges of the triangle.

9 When you are happy with your design, carefully unfold the snowflake. Flatten your snowflake by placing it under a heavy book for a few minutes.

Templates for Halloween Silhouettes

These templates are printed at half the original size we used to make the silhouettes. Ask an adult to help you set the photocopier to copy them at 200%—this will make them twice the size. However, if you prefer to have smaller silhouettes, you can just trace them off the page (or copy them at 100%).

Index

allspice 101
apron, T-shirt 14–16
arm warmer, sock 114–15

baking soda 23
balls, sponge 46–7
bananas 83
bark 110
baskets, spring 24–5
bats 81
bicarbonate of soda see baking soda
bird feeder 32–3
bookmarks 75
buried treasure 44

candy cane chocolate bark 110–11
cardboard rolls 32, 112–13
    flower craft 40–1
    spooky 76–8
caterpillars 55
ceramics 71
cereal 73
cinnamon mats 100–1
coffee 66
coldest day ever recorded 119
contact paper 87
cork 91
cornflour see cornstarch
cornstarch 65
cotton 67
cotton balls 54
    sheep 30–1
crayon art 48–9

découpage 27, 122
    tiles 26–7
desk organizer, tissue-box 112–13

eyeball wreath 88–89
eyes 89

food coloring 60, 64
file holder, cereal box 72–3
fleece 118
flower craft, cardboard roll 40–1
fruit
    halloween 82–4
    kebabs 42–3

gift in a jar 120–1
glass 120
greeting cards, bookmarks 74–5

halloween
    fruit 82–4

silhouettes 80–1, 127
    wreath 88–9
handkerchiefs 113
handprint
    snowman 98–9
    tree 20–1
hats, easy no-sew 118–19
hearts 103
jars, gift in 120–1
    jar lid magnets 122–3
jewelry box, shoe-box 92–3
juice boxes 104

kebabs, fruit 42–3
key chain, T-shirt 94–5

learning skills 6

magazines 56
magnets, jar lid 122–3
mat, woven magazine 56–8
mats, no-sew cinnamon 100–1
melons 43
memo board, ribbon 90–1
metals 123
minerals 109
money box 79
monsters 34
mugs
    permanent marker 70–1
    sock mug warmer 116–17
Muppets 37
music boxes 63

nail polish 11
necklaces, washer 10–11
newspaper art 52–3
no-sew projects
    cinnamon mats 100
    fleece hat 118

paper 12
    chain people 12–13
    snowflakes 124–6
patio paint 64–5
photos 36
piggy banks 79
popsicles, homemade 50–1
potato stamp stationery 28–9
pudding 50
pumpkins 77
puppets, family photo 36–7

ribbon 90
rock art 59

rocks, painted 59

salt dough 107–9
sheep, cotton ball 30–1
shoe boxes 93
silhouettes, halloween 80–1, 127
snowflakes, paper 124–6
snowmen
    handprints 98–9
    juice box 104–6
socks 115
    arm warmer 114–15
    caterpillar 54–5
    gym bag buddies 22–3
    monsters 34–5
    mug warmer 116–17
sponge balls 46–7
sponges 47
spooky cardboard rolls 76–8
spring basket 24–5
stationery, potato stamp 28–9
sticky-backed plastic 87
sunflower seeds 33

T-shirts 95
    apron 14–16
    food coloring tie-dye 60–1
    key chain 94–5
    music player holder 62–3
tags, backpack 85–7
tank top, coffee and tea stained 66–7
tea 17, 66
tea card, Think of Me 17–19
templates 127
tie-dye T-shirt 60–1
tiles, découpage 26–7
tips 7
toilet paper 41
toilet roll tubes see cardboard rolls
top hats 99
treasure map 44–5
tree, handprint 20–1
trees 20

valentines, 3D 102–3

washers 10
wax crayons 49
weaving 57
wool 117
wreath, eyeball 88–9

yogurt container 24, 30, 52, 64, 98, 122